THE ART OF BEING

A Well Dressed Wife

Anne Fogarty

V&A Publishing

❧❧❧❧❧❧❧❧❧❧❧❧❧❧❧❧❧❧❧❧❧❧❧❧❧❧❧❧❧❧❧❧❧❧❧❧❧

The Art of Being A Well-Dressed Wife was written by American fashion designer Anne Fogarty (1919–1980) in 1959. Fogarty designed for Margot Inc., Saks Fifth Avenue and her own label, Anne Fogarty Inc. She won numerous awards including the Coty American Fashion Critics Award and the Neiman Marcus Award. Her designs can be seen at the Costume Institute at the Metropolitan Museum of Art.

❧❧❧❧❧❧❧❧❧❧❧❧❧❧❧❧❧❧❧❧❧❧❧❧❧❧❧❧❧❧❧❧❧❧❧❧❧

First published in 1959
This edition published by V&A Publishing, 2011
V&A Publishing
Victoria and Albert Museum
South Kensington
London SW7 2RL
www.vandapublishing.com

Book design and compilation copyright © V&A Publishing, 2011

The moral right of the author has been asserted.

ISBN 978 1 85177 630 6

10 9 8 7 6 5 4 3 2
2015 2014 2013

Design by **here** www.heredesign.co.uk
Black and White photography by John French © V&A Images

Printed in China

V&A Publishing

Supporting the world's leading
museum of art and design,
the Victoria and Albert
Museum, London

Contents

Wife-Dressing

'If you adore her, you must adorn her. There lies the essence of a happy marriage'

A WORD TO HUSBANDS: *If you adore her, you must adorn her. There lies the essence of a happy marriage.*

WIFE-DRESSING is many things:
An art.
A science.
A labour of love.
A means of self-expression.
And, above all, a contributing factor to a happy marriage.

Wife-dressing begins with the traditional rings for your third finger, left hand. From that point on, it's up to you to interpret your changed role in society. The clothes you choose and the way you choose to wear them will state very clearly your outlook on life in general and your attitude towards life as a wife in particular.

Wife-dressing applies to all married women, from brides brushing the rice from their hair to veteran homemakers and career mothers who may want to pause and re-evaluate their wardrobes. Wife-dressing has nothing to do with age. If you're old enough to have a husband and young enough to want his admiration, you're a candidate for wife-dressing and the rewards that go with it.

While the bachelor girl can be a chameleon, forever changing herself over to suit a new whim, a new job, or a new beau, the wife has moved on to better things. She has found her cozy corner and the man she wants to share it with. What she must do next is decide how best to dramatize her new role and crystallize her position in terms of her home, her husband, her job if she has one, her friends and business associates.

I have been married for 16 years and, despite having worked at a career all that time, I still think of myself first and foremost as a wife. My career as a designer has perhaps made me more aware of clothes and their subtleties of meaning than women with other professional interests. Yet, with all the pressures of the fashion world and worries about where the waistline should be *next* season, I have come to one durable principle that is timeless.

When your husband's eyes
light up as he comes in at
night, you're in sad shape if
it's only because he smells
dinner cooking.

The first principle of wife-dressing is Complete Femininity – the selection of clothes as an *adornment*, not as a mere covering.

The most dangerous threat to successful wife-dressing is the triumphant cry, 'I'm married! The battle is won!'

To paraphrase John Paul Jones: 'You have not yet begun to fight.'

The wedding ring is only the beginning. When your husband's eyes light up as he comes in at night, you're in sad shape if it's only because he smells dinner cooking.

Most men claim to be indifferent to fashion, if not downright afraid. They can contemplate outer space without blinking an eye, cross polar ice packs on top and underneath, even walk into a darkened cellar where you've heard noises – yet the mention of fashions or a shopping trip turns them pale and trembling.

Why this is I don't know. Maybe it goes back to Adam and Eve. Or maybe Freud can tell us. One thing is clear: However much your husband may disdain fashion, however many times he may mumble something incomprehensible when you ask his advice, he is getting your message. Instinctively he will respond to every facet of wife-dressing whether you're being the hostess, the maid-of-all-work, or the devastating creature curled up on the sofa with a Midnight Snack for Two.

Like married life itself, wife-dressing is pretty basic. It requires frank understanding of yourself, a healthy attitude towards your new responsibilities, a willingness to learn from experience, and a buoyant elation about being alive.

If I had to boil down my thinking about clothes into one word, that word would be DISCIPLINE – of the mind, the body, and the emotions.

DISCIPLINE makes you the woman you are rather than a hodgepodge of everyone else's ideas chosen without consideration of your own colouring and proportions. Fashion ideas are meant to be copied and borrowed, but be careful in your selection. It's a little like borrowing clothes, something you wouldn't dream of doing from someone whose looks you admire but whose type is no more yours than the man in the moon.

DISCIPLINE results in a clear-cut picture of your own identity as a person. It is easier to clothe a clear-cut image than a hazy mirage. You are you. You are not the model in that photograph or the girl beside you in an elevator or a woman eating lunch at the next table. What they are wearing may stop traffic, but be sure it's right for you before emulating the effect.

DISCIPLINE is the secret to good grooming, well-cared for clothes, an organized household, and the seemingly effortless success of a marriage.

DISCIPLINE stops you from buying an unbecoming coat because it's a bargain.

DISCIPLINE prevents you from deluding yourself that a hem is right when you're too lazy to straighten it.

DISCIPLINE makes you a stickler for details which, unchecked, can add up to a monster-size catastrophe.

But please don't confuse discipline with hardness or calculation. Look around you and you'll see that the most delightfully casual women are those who know exactly what they're doing and why. It can take longer time and more care to be a windblown child of nature than bandbox perfect, but if that's how you want to look, self-discipline will help you devote the time and trouble to it.

This book will cover many aspects of wife-dressing, but to begin with, here are some of my pet theories on the subject in general:

A GENERAL GUIDE TO WIFE-DRESSING

1. Compress your wardrobe

Be relentless. If it's out of style, makes you itch or squirm with discomfort, turns your skin sallow – get rid of it fast!

Unless you have a cedar-lined attic or more cupboard space than I've ever seen in the biggest household, don't hang on to things that may someday come back into style, you think might look okay if you change your hair style or bought a complete new set of accessories, has sentimental value and the teardrop stains to remind you, or that's good enough for the rain or wearing around the house.

Fashion is for today. Don't look back. Don't look further ahead than the current season. Don't save the dress that won you

Nothing spoils an outfit more than time-worn shoes.

wolf whistles summer before last. The whistles may change to groans. Don't buy something at the end of season to wear the following year. End-of-season bargains can boomerang.

Sentiment may cast a rosy glow on a certain little something your husband admired on a special occasion. You may want to keep it *always* – but *always* can end quickly where fashion is concerned, and all of a sudden you may look like last year's rotogravure.

With the dross and fool's gold cleared away, the real nuggets shine. An uncluttered wardrobe gives you a working knowledge of what you have and full control over selections. Endless hangers squashed together are not only confusing but hard on the clothes themselves. In your confusion you may take the easy way out and keep wearing the same three or four things rather than plough through the great unknown. It's better to have fewer clothes, all wearable and each accessorized in your mind so that when you put something on you know at once which shoes and gloves you're going to wear. Complete costume planning is possible only with an intimate awareness of all your clothes.

2. Weeding is a money-saver

I'm talking about actual dollars-and-cents savings. Collect your discards, and if you don't have favourite people such as a sister or cousin or niece who can wear them, do one of two things. Sell them to a dealer in used clothing such as the very chic thrift shops that have sprung up in many of the big cities. Or, give them to a social organization.

3. Old shoes must go

Old soldiers may fade away; old Garbo movies may make you cry – but old shoes are only good for hanging on the back of a bridal car or giving to the children for dress-up play. Nothing spoils an outfit more than time-worn shoes and shoes which are obviously out of style. Heel shapes and vamp cuts change gradually from season to season, but the change becomes glaringly obvious when a three year-old pair comes out of the shoe bag.

Since shoes are made in such an enormous range of colour, fabric and type, don't buy them to last for ever. Exceptions are active sports shoes, such as golf shoes, sneakers, and moccasins, which take a lot of punishment.

I always have more shoes than dresses, with different colour shoes giving new life to various ensembles. I am hard on my shoes and by the end of their fashion usefulness they're about ready for the dust bin. Those that are wearable but no longer suitable are sent off with discarded clothes.

Old shoes should not be worn as house shoes or bedroom slippers. They lack both the proper support and good looks. You will feel better and look better in appropriate footwear.

As for expense, my feeling about shoes is the same I have about other clothes. If you feel guilty about spending lots on shoes, spend a little less on each pair but replenish more frequently. Fashion is a living, changing part of your life.

4. The skeletal jewel box

It may be pleasant to dig your hands into an overstuffed jewel box while visions of pirate treasure pass through your mind. It is an idle fantasy. Despite the exploits of international play-girls, my feeling is the best jewel box is the one that is sparsely filled. Not being able to see the wood for the trees is the chief woe of the overstuffed jewel cask. You won't be able to find what you want. The chain of one bracelet will be snarled in some earrings. The prongs of a pin will scratch the smooth patina of a medallion. In your haste or annoyance you may break something valuable or wear the wrong jewellery.

Few of us have more than a few pieces of valuable jewellery and these are kept apart. But like the rest of your wardrobe, your costume jewellery collection should be kept to a skeletal minimum, subject to constant replenishment. The reason is simple. Why panic over making a choice among 12 pairs of gold earrings, some of which are scratched or dulled? One or two fresh pairs is enough. Rhinestones are lovely and among my favourite adornments, but let's face it: they lose their lustre and cannot be cleaned.

If you're really crazy about one particular piece of costume jewellery, such as a gold-plated pin, investigate the possibility of having it copied in real gold. This way you can build your collection of real jewellery in designs you have tested and like.

5. Excess accessories

Another case of the Confusion of Profusion is too many scarves, belts, gloves, and handbags, and by 'too many' I mean

relics of former years which keep getting in the way of the accessories currently in use. Admittedly, most accessories can be worn indefinitely because classic styles change very little. If an accessory hasn't been worn for a year, if it's shabby, if the colour is faded or doesn't go with anything you have, if you simply can't stand to wear it – that's right, out it goes. And you'd be surprised how much fresher and easier to use your remaining accessories will seem with all the deadwood cleared away.

6. Shop in a shopping mood

The worst mistake you can make is to force yourself to shop. To idly decide it's spring, the bird's on the wing, is not the time for a foray on the stores UNLESS you're in a truly shopping mood. The most important part of shopping is your frame of mind. How can you make a proper choice if you feel like the mistreated heroine of a soap opera?

A frivolous hat or other bit of forbidden fruit are ideal for beating the blues, but stay out of the dress and coat departments until you feel enthusiastic. If your body isn't attuned to fashion, you won't look right in anything. And if you're depressed because you've gained a few pounds, don't buy something too small to grow down to. Lose the few pounds first and then go shopping. *Remember, diets always start tomorrow.*

One thing that makes me really bristle is the subject of dressing to go shopping. Suburbanites are the worst offenders. How can you possibly see what a dress will do for you if your hair is in pins under a kerchief, your face devoid of make-up, your girdle left home in the drawer? I am continually astounded to see young wives, especially, shopping in jeans or shorts, trying on cocktail dresses with saddle shoes, murmuring into the mirror, 'Well, of course, I'll be wearing a different bra and my hair will be swept into a French knot and . . .'

And . . . that explains why so many clothes are such a big disappointment when they are finally worn. The wearer had no clear idea of how the dress would look with her underpinnings, shoes, and jewellery and hair done because she 'visualized' the final effect in flat shoes and her hair in a pony tail.

This is one reason for my next point:

7. Dress for everything

From early morning to late at night, dress actively for whatever you are doing. Don't wear an ageing cocktail dress to the office or a 'beat-up' wool for housework. Their original design was for something quite different and they will be uncomfortable as well as unattractive.

I've covered the reasons for dressing properly to go shopping. I've explained my feelings about old shoes; add to that decrepit hats for the rain. Rain can be pretty romantic. Why look like a drowned scarecrow when you can be a touch of sunshine on a dark day in perky rainwear?

For working around the house, wear practical, comfortable work-pants, cotton coveralls, or dresses in washable fabrics and shoes to give your feet solid support. For the office, wear understated, simple clothes in comfortable fabrics and styles that retain their lines after a full day's activity. For at-home leisure, wear glamorous, feminine lounge coats, long-skirted dresses, gay coveralls, or lavish pants and tops. Negligees are for the boudoir *only!* For social occasions, dress carefully for each occasion, keeping in mind the special role you will play as wife, hostess, or member of your community.

Study your clothing needs as carefully as you furnish your home. If you live in a cold climate, have a collection of boots in various colours and heel heights so that you can be warm all winter and still not look like a lumberjack.

If you give small, informal dinner parties, have a few long or short colourful skirts and dresses in jersey or flannel with gay party aprons to make your role of hostess festive yet comfortable.

If your husband's work means continuous parties, conventions, and entertainment, pep up your collection of after-five clothes with satin pumps in different colours.

These are a few of my thoughts as I plunge into the many facets of wife-dressing. There are only two more suggestions before I begin:

One: Stand before a full-length, triple-view mirror with a strong, honest light. Take a good look at yourself from every angle.

Two: Decide how you can improve your physical proportions to fit the image you have of yourself AND choose the kind of 'look' you want to convey as a wife, an example of which is my own choice of pared-down naturalness with emphasis on contour and colour.

Know who you are, what you stand for – your enthusiasms, your ambitions, your hopes, your responsibilities. Remember that it's your husband for whom you're dressing. Keep him in mind when you shop. No matter how much your best friends like something, if your husband is critical you'll find yourself giving it up, even if you're sure *you* know more than he does about women's clothes.

It may take a little while for you as a complete, unique individual to emerge, but it's all up to you and the fascinating business of **WIFE-DRESSING**.

❧ ❧ ❧

Breaking the Rules

*'I have worn a red moleskin coat over
a dinner dress to an elegant night club
and felt more gala than the minks and
chinchillas surrounding me'*

A WORD TO HUSBANDS: The finest scarf or collar made
To keep a woman warm
By night or day or sea or land
Is still a lover's arm.

W. H. DAVIES

This is a perfect and poetic example of substituting your personal choice of neck-warmer.

A. F.

If you must be a slave to something, make it Scrabble or knitting or casserole cookery. Anything but fashion, where you must be the mistress of your fate.

Don't be fooled. Don't be cajoled. Don't be 'conned'. Don't let the mythical 'they' who supposedly dictate fashion from above squash your individuality. As a designer, I am one of the 'they'. I believe in fashion rules because they work. I also believe in breaking the rules as an *elaboration* on proven dogma. Don't throw the rules away. Work from them. There's an analogy in abstract painting: you can't be a successful modern unless you've mastered traditional forms. In fashion you need wide knowledge of fabrics, textures, and lines if you're going off on your own interpretation. If you have this knowledge, don't be afraid.

Fashion is too free, too creative an expression of yourself, to be confined by inflexible dogma. Just as cosmetics are an improvement on nature, so is your interpretation of current fashion an improvement of your personal appearance.

Colour is one way to break the rules. While 'basic black' is chic for town, try it for the country – but be sure it's tweed. Wear white in the city in winter. You will create a glow of gaiety and lightness in drab surroundings.

Have an open mind about colour. Because a nearsighted aunt once said you looked sickly in green at the age of ten, maybe you've banished green from your colour spectrum for life.

Skin tones change. What was wrong, wrong, wrong ten years ago may transform you into a radiant beauty now. Aside from which, colour is a matter of shading. Forest green may darken the shadows under your eyes. Apple green will cast a sunny reflection on your cheeks.

As a matter of fact there is no colour you cannot wear! Why? Because colour suitability is governed by your skin tones, and with today's enormous range of powder bases and skin foundations, you can change your skin tone at will and wear any fashion shade you like.

Never close your mind to a colour. Remember, too, that texture is an important element. The same dress in the same shade of red may look wonderful on you in soft velvet but too harsh in a hard-finished taffeta. Think in terms of colour combined with texture, not of one or the other independently.

SOME FASHION RULES TO BREAK

'Never dress your child in black'

Do dress your little girl in black if her satiny skin and pixie eyes will take on a Renaissance glow from the colour usually reserved for adults. A good example is a velvet party dress, smocked high across the bodice and topped with a white Peter Pan collar.

'Tweeds are for the country'

I love tweeds for cocktails in town, and I don't mean barging in with a pleated skirt and hacking jacket. I do mean something that will be a wonderful change from traditional cocktail wear, perhaps a thin pastel tweed styled with a deep décolletage and a full or slim skirt, adorned with formalized jewellery such as chunky gold bracelets or a jungle of beads picking up the tweed colours.

'Drip-dries are the only thing for travel'

Take drip-dries by all means, but also include your favourite silk blouse and frothy negligee even if you have to bring them home dirty. Travel should enrich you, not deny your sensibilities.

'Fur bags are for winter'

I like to carry a small fur bag with cottons or silks in summer. Also, an enormous, shaggy tote-bag is amusing and durable for week-end travel and will take more punishment than a straw or fabric carry-all.

'Patent leather means spring, black kid means autumn'

The sparkle and vigour of patent leather puts it in my year-round wardrobe. Its shiny brightness adds zing to woollens and tweeds as well as cottons and silks, whether the temperature is 10 or 110. As for black kid, I'm not wild about black shoes anyway, but in summer with a dark-coloured dress and a deep tan on my legs, I can think of no better change of pace than neat black kid pumps.

'Fun furs should be limited to casual wear'

Furs should be judged by their styling, not their intrinsic value. I have worn a red moleskin coat over a dinner dress to an elegant night club and felt more gala than the minks and chinchillas surrounding me.

'Never mix real jewellery with costume'

Whether to mix them depends on three things: Styling. Size. Colour. I often wear a real gold pin with a costume bracelet, a real diamond circlet with a matching rhinestone bangle. It is not the intrinsic harmony but the total and *tonal* effect that counts.

A good rule for breaking the rules is: When fabrics are conventional, run riot with colour. When colours behave, run wild with texture. Good taste and sound judgment alone must guide your decisions. There are no inflexibilities in fashion. MOOD and MOTIVE set the pace. New styles are a point of departure. You're not supposed to look exactly like everyone else, as if you were all wearing the uniforms of a chic army.

Good taste will stop you from wearing mink shorts or from buying them in the first place. Sound judgment will tell you when you can entertain guests in gold lamé pants and a Byronic silk shirt and when to confine your exuberance to an organza apron over a floor-length jersey.

MOOD is hard to pin down. It's in the same category as 'Which came first – the chicken or the egg?' Whether clothes create a mood or vice-versa is often interchangeable. Let's just say that mood and clothes are closely entwined. So be careful. If you're feeling depressed, don't try to jazz up your spirits with too violent an extreme so that you wind up looking like Pagliacci, your sadness intensified by the brightness of your costume.

Bright colours are stimulating, true, but take it easy! Perk yourself up with a shocking-pink hat *or* an orange scarf *or* a chartreuse belt *or* sunshine-yellow gloves. A touch of gaiety will do a trick. An avalanche will bury you. If it's a rainy day, wear a yellow slicker or carry a floral-patterned umbrella that the daylight can seep through.

For the great big world outside, moods take on a more subtle flavour. Some days you may feel fettered, tied down, straining to be free. Those are the days to wear a dress that won't constrict. Don't weigh yourself down. Necklaces and bracelets without which you normally feel naked should be left at home.

Judgment is another way of saying, 'Stop and think'. You may look great in your dressing-room mirror, but is what you're wearing appropriate for what you'll be doing? High heels will not help you climb over seats at a football game. Beige silk shoes will sink into muddy turf at a golf tournament. An enormous straw hat will wind up on the floor of an open car. A warm wool, however chic, may suffocate you in a hot theatre or a crowded club.

Judgment also prevents you from wearing a dress you're unsure of to an important gathering where that uncertainty will hinder your personal success.

MOTIVES are more a matter of cool calculation. Women are by nature supposed to be calculating creatures, but my feeling is that there isn't enough calculation in planning their wardrobes.

It's strange but many women will spend endless time and give deep thought to menus, furnishings, vacation plans, and the like. But when it comes to their own clothes and grooming, to the picture they present to the world, they ad-lib, make it up as they go along, search wildly for the right hat ten minutes before attending a wedding, dig through masses of shoes and gloves for something that will go with the dress they have on.

The wife plays an increasingly important role in the advancement of her husband, especially in big industry and the professions.

Your clothes should express value without extravagance, warmth without being brazen, and understanding without looking like Whistler's Mother.

Many large organizations have developed a system for interviewing executives' wives, especially when promotions to high-echelon jobs are in the offing.

In any social situation, remember that you are an appendage of your husband, Adam's rib that was separated from him to form woman and now spiritually returned to his side.

It will take some clever appraisal on your part, but your clothes should express value without extravagance, warmth without being brazen, and understanding without looking like Whistler's Mother.

Much the same point applies to any situation of stress or uncertainty. A conference with your child's teacher. Making a speech at a community luncheon. Or meeting anyone who is important to your own or your husband's way of life.

To sum up, fashion rules may be broken, moods expressed, motives clearly thought out and acted upon accordingly.

Let your consciousness – of yourself and all about you – be your guide.

❦ ❦ ❦

THREE

You Can't Go Home Again

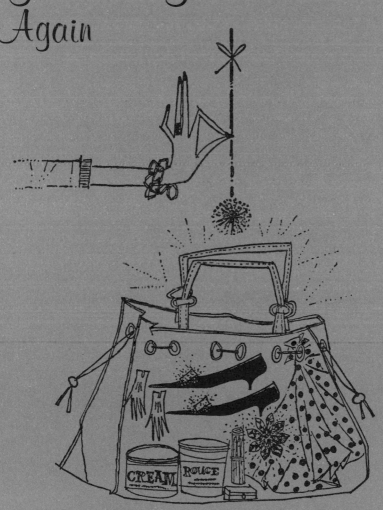

Urbia, suburbia, exurbia, wherever you live, whatever the climate, wife-dressing should echo the Scouts' motto, 'Be Prepared!'

Think beyond the dressing-room mirror. Will you be away all day? All evening? Just a few hours? Is it going to rain? Get very warm? Turn cold? Are you going to be sitting down a lot? Walking your feet off? A combination of both?

In this context, wife-dressing is like a military exercise. You must develop your survival instincts and be fully prepared to meet both the expected – and the unexpected. What you're aiming for is a combination of self-containment and mobility. You want adaptability in what you're wearing and freedom of movement. You can have all these advantages at your fingertips by carrying a tote-bag – which I sincerely believe is the best thing that's happened to women since the vote.

I think of my oversized pouch as a kind of conjurer's bag full of magical tricks that help me preserve my appearance and change it at will. I always carry a small clutch bag in the tote for quick errands away from the office or to go out for lunch.

On an average morning I may start out in a shirt-dress with a convertible collar, medium-heel shoes for the workroom, clean white shortie gloves, and my current favourite jangle bracelet on one wrist. Comes noon, I want to look fresh for a lunch date with my husband and some business associates of his – so out of the tote comes a pair of my highest heel patent pumps, a diamond pin to wear on the convertible neckline, a pair of fresh white gloves, and a small patent bag for the few things I'll need at lunch.

I always carry extra white gloves and extra stockings.

While this is an example of a career wife, a more domesticated friend of mine who lives in the wilds of Westchester has adapted the technique to meet the demands of her life. About once a week she hires a babysitter to guard the home front and comes to New York to do errands, exchange gossip with friends over lunch, and eventually pick up her husband at his office for an evening on the town.

Her problem is a common one. How can she spend all day shopping, be elegant at lunch with her friends, and appear shiny as a new penny when it comes time to take her husband's mind off business? She doesn't want to be improperly dressed for any of these diverse activities; nor does she want to cart a suitcase for one day in the city.

I discussed these points with her and here is her tote-plot for such a day. She has a bright red-and-gold-checked knit dress which she wears with a solid red coat lined in the knit fabric. It's her favourite go-to-town ensemble because she starts out with red kid pumps, gold jersey gloves and gold jewellery, and a dark gold felt hat, which makes her smartly dressed and comfortable on the train and to do her errands, shop, and meet friends for lunch.

In the evening she digs into the tote for her metamorphosis, coming up with red satin sandals that match the dress and immediately remove it from the daytime category, a diamond pin and thin diamond bracelet to replace the gold, and white kid shorties instead of gold jersey gloves.

With these few changes she has achieved a duality of purpose that suits perfectly what she is doing. The checked knit dress with satin and diamond (or rhinestone) accessories can go to the theatre or an elegant restaurant or cocktail party in tasteful if understated elegance.

This might be a good place to sound off against that perennial stand-by, the 'basic black' as the backbone of a changing wardrobe. I think that concept belongs to a different era. My mother used to have a basic black dress, which she wore with outlandish hats. In a modern wardrobe a black dress is an 'important' dress, but should not be considered the all dual-purpose wear.

In planning an outfit that will take you through a whole day and into the evening with the aid and comfort of 'tote-ables', think in terms of greys, beiges, and gold in combination with bright colours for accent. Patterns and checks lend themselves well to change.

Self confidence, rightly or wrongly, lies in cosmetics.

It might be said that TOTE-THINKING is tantamount to TOTAL THINKING, getting into the habit of planning ahead with intelligence and imagination.

Another important application of the tote principle is in going to parties, especially when they're a distance from home and, most especially, if the weather is bad. Why arrive with a brave little smile and mud all over your pretty brocaded shoes from squishing up a muddy driveway when you can wear your boots and tote your shoes?

On trips, too, the tote is a blessing because you keep it right with you. On a train. In a plane. In a car. Comfort and relaxation are essential if you are to look your best on arrival at your destination. Carry in your tote a pair of soft ballet slippers or collapsible scuffs to slip on while travelling. On page 87 I discuss travel at length, but if your way of life makes this a regular event, keep shoe socks or cellophane bags handy for covering your shoes so they won't smudge anything else in the bag.

Once you've acquired the tote habit, you will adapt its uses for many personal needs, finding it indispensable for a shopping junket with the children, the day you spend reading to patients at the hospital, the morning that finds you at the supermarket, the dressmaker, and picking up the laundry.

There are no limits as to what may or may not be toted. One of my models is a stickler about make-up. When she can't wash her face after work and apply completely new make-up, she has a miserable evening, convinced she looks awful. Her tote-bag is a portable dressing table. She takes the trouble to fit it out with small pots of her creams and bases and powders and pencils and mascaras and nail polish, all of which surprisingly take up very little room, having been organized for the purpose.

Now she never worries about an impromptu dinner date or laughing so hard at a movie that her mascara runs. Self-confidence, rightly or wrongly, lies in cosmetics. She carries her self-confidence around with her within easy reach, as can you, in a tote-bag.

Another model carries a co-ordinated scarf, gloves, and lipstick in the same shade for a mid-day change of character or 'in case I feel like being a different person all of a sudden'. With a tote-bag you need never ardently wish you could go home for a few minutes to change your gloves or add another bit of adornment.

Fashion models originated the tote idea. I think they are the epitome of modern women with busy lives who want to look beautiful and feel beautiful all the time. Since fashion is their profession, a lot can be learned from studying their habits and thinking.

Quite another element of not being able to go home and having to be ready for anything is what I call THE TRAPS – the diabolical pitfalls which are nobody's fault but often can be side-stepped by thinking ahead. Fashion traps have ruined more evenings for women than anything I can think of, including the disaster of coming face to face with someone wearing the same dress!

THE TRAPS are lying in wait for you. Here's how to avoid the more common ones and alert your senses to new and different traps which may even now be in the experimental stage.

1. Wearing a tight, narrow dress to a buffet party

Don't! because the one word 'buffet' means that you may wind up sitting on the floor, folding yourself up like a collapsible drinking cup, and easing your tightly encased body down on a low, low pillow, your legs thrust awkwardly before you and your body awkwardly rigid because of the constricting lines which looked so great when you were standing up. Eating will be impossible in this position and all those bantering stories you were saving will stop, frozen, on your stiff lips while your husband asks, 'What's the matter, dear, aren't you hungry?'

Of course you don't *have to* sit on the floor, but you may find yourself slightly isolated, perched on a chair a couple of feet higher than the other diners.

Save very tight dresses for stand-up parties or receptions or dinner parties where you can count on sitting at a table.

Next time you're invited to dinner and you want to wear something that fits like a sausage skin and requires a mince-footed slither for locomotion, your only way is to call your hostess first and find out the seating arrangements. If she's planning floor-service, make your plans floor-serviceable with a full-skirted dress that will enable you to sit cross-legged within its folds on the floor or straddle a bench or stretch out halfway down the playroom steps with a plate of slippery food and a goblet of wine perfectly balanced.

2. Not knowing how dressy or undressy everyone is going to be

The English language doesn't seem to cover this situation, so calling your hostess is no good. Save the call. She'll only say something vague that won't tell you a thing.

'Informal' to some people means corduroys; to others, no decorations will be worn.

Somewhere in between will be the indefinable criterion for the party. If you worry about overdressing, choose something in a covered-up style and depend on an unusual colour or fabric texture for drama and gaiety and exquisite jewellery for elegance. Conservatism with dash is the best combination for an evening's journey into the 'unknown'.

Another approach is the dress-and-jacket concept. Informal with the jacket on; formal with the jacket off.

One caution here is not to consider every dress-and-jacket costume suitable for party wear unless it's planned for dual purpose. Some costumes are planned for day wear only, with a casual dress beneath the casual jacket. Others in taffeta or satin are strictly after-five and should not be worn to the office however covered up they are.

A good example of dual purpose is a grey flannel costume I have which looks like a suit with the jacket on. But underneath there is a white satin embroidered bodice that can go to cocktails or the theatre with the jacket over my shoulders or folded over my arm.

While I adore the dress-and-jacket look, I think it is easier to depend on accessories for dressing it up or down than on the actual styling of the garment. Simplicity is the key to dual-purpose dressing, plus the imagination to add the right touches for the right effect.

3. Not planning for small emergencies

Why court disaster of the kind that plagues you regularly? For instance, if you are a chronic button-popper or heel-in-hem catcher, keep in your bag one of those tiny sewing kits the size of a penny. That way you don't have to ask your hostess for needle and thread or, if you're out, suffer through the rest of the evening feeling conspicuous.

Most of us suffer from some sort of chronic ill, such as sinus headaches. If you do, don't count on finding the exact brand of Aspirin that you prefer. Have a few of your own in a tiny pillbox. There are so many pretty ones today. Protect your husband's enjoyment in this way too. If he's feeling miserable, so will you.

4. Forgetting the icy winds of summer air-conditioning

There is no more miserable trap than walking through a door on a hot summer evening in your gossamer bareness into what feels like the return of the Ice Age. Air-conditioning is a benevolent evil. We don't know what we'd do without it. Yet we're miserable much of the time with it because our teeth are chattering and we're freezing to death.

Summer means air-conditioned theatres, restaurants, office buildings. Units at home can be regulated, but elsewhere you're at other people's mercies.

Beat the heat, and avoid chilblains too, by *always* having a cover up with you in summer. Designers have recognized the growing problem of air-conditioned offices, shops, and restaurants, where the temperature can drop as much as 50 degrees between the outside and inside. Abundantly available are lovely cashmere and lamb's-wool sweaters and shrugs in soft summer colours for daytime wear.

For evening, if you're going out bare-shouldered, you're not correctly dressed for either town or country unless you have something to cover you. Fancy sweaters, embroidered, beaded, or trimmed with fur, can be elegant if not overdone. Also shawls and stoles, crocheted or in fabric, as well as summer coats in cotton or silk.

Cotton jackets in floral prints are marvellous cover-ups because they can be worn with shorts, slacks, skirts, and slim-lined cocktail wear.

Don't find yourself *in* in the cold. In summer, prepare for the indoor refrigerator while planning for the outdoor furnace.

5. Not listening to the plans carefully

I've done it so often I'm ashamed. We went to an indoor night polo match and I wore an outfit heavy enough for winter at the Polo Grounds. We went to a summer concert in Central Park, but it never occurred to me that I'd be sitting on damp grass against a very hard tree.

Pay attention to plans and translate them in your own mind into what will be the best thing to wear in terms of temperature, atmosphere, and physical activity.

6. The treacherous night air

Small hotels in mountain and seaside resorts often don't have heat at night. Always take two robes on vacations, one of them warm.

People who entertain you on terraces or back patios on summer evenings are used to the fact that it's chillier under those trees or up on the twelfth floor facing east. You may be cooler than you think. Take a cover-up.

Driving back from places at night is cooler than going places in the first place, so put an extra sweater on the back seat.

In addition to foreseeable traps, there are the unforeseeable emergencies, the sudden crises you may not be able to avoid but where a little first aid will help. Use ingenuity:

1. IF the top button comes off your coat. For example, several years ago, just as Tom and I were leaving the apartment for a football game, I discovered that the top button of a tweed coat was not only off but missing. There were no two ways about it. I wanted to wear that tweed coat. I couldn't decide what to do until I suddenly remembered an enormous gold safety pin I had given Tom some time before. He didn't like to wear it because it dug holes in his ties, and since it was all in the family I took back the pin. Fastening the top of my coat, it not only added a distinctive accessory note but has since become a fashion-accepted piece of jewellery. It has become something of a personal trademark for me because I never tire of wearing it or including it as an accessory to my collections.

Don't think I'm suggesting that every household or pocket contains a gold safety pin. What does suggest itself is the availability of ingenious thinking in fashion emergencies. When something goes wrong, don't panic. As the boys at IBM say, THINK!

2. IF an overfriendly sheep-dog has cuddled you and left a trail of fuzz on your black dress or a small child has crushed biscuits on your shoulder, take a deep breath and make haste for the nearest roll of Scotch Tape, which is usually available wherever you are. Incidentally, it's a good idea to keep a roll in

Have your utensils with you. They won't do you any good at home. Grooming is a continuing job, so you can continue to be well-dressed.

the glove compartment of your car as well as in your tote-bag.

Wrap some tape, sticky side out, several times around your knuckles until you have a tape knuckle-duster that will pick up anything loose on fabric. This also works on suede shoes, belts, and handbags.

There are many compact grooming aids on the market suitable for carrying around with you as required. There are tiny clothes brushes the size of match books, suede brushes in cases, and, recently introduced, a battery-run vacuum brush the size of a small flashlight and very lightweight.

Have your utensils with you. They won't do you any good at home. Grooming is a continuing job, so you can continue to be well-dressed.

3. IF you've snagged a stocking and haven't an emergency pair with you, take it off and reverse it. The run will shift to the inside of your leg and be less noticeable. But always try to have a spare pair with you. They weigh nothing – and in an emergency are worth their weight in gold.

4. IF you've lost or forgotten your lipstick, wash the remaining lipstick off, then apply foundation or powder to your mouth to give it a smooth surface. Then using a clean fingertip, apply rouge to your lips, or some lipstick taken from the side of someone else's tube. The rouge is much better because it is a colour that suits your own complexion.

5. IF, as sometimes happens, a buttonhole keeps slipping off the button at a strategic spot on the bodice, twist a small rubber band under the button. It will be unnoticeable and the rubbery texture will adhere to the fabric at least until you get home.

FOUR

After the Trousseau, What?

A WORD TO HUSBANDS:	*'Has a woman who knew she was well-dressed ever caught cold? No!'*

F. W. NIETZSCHE

If you're a recent bride, you have a wedding costume, a going-away ensemble, and a mass of oddments in tissue paper lavished on you at various showers and pow-wows. Now that the shouting is over, your hair de-riced, and the thank-you's written, your first duty is to set your wardrobe as well as your household in order.

Here, then, is a Fashion Framework of wardrobe requirements for wife-dressing which might be a working guide for you as a bride as well as a basis for reassessment if you are a wife whose trousseau has long since worn out.

Let's begin with the most basic of basic essentials:

HOSIERY

Buying stockings by the dozen pairs is far and away the most practical system since you can match up strays indefinitely and since stockings generally sell for less by the box than by individual pairs. This is not an extravagance for basic stockings, and can actually be a big saving.

For coloured stockings or other hosiery fads, don't go overboard with quantity. Try two pairs at the most. Stocking colours are extremely personal and look different according to skin tone.

In planning your regular stocking supply, select two distinct shades, depending on your favourite fashion colours. One should be on the beige side to go with browns, reds, tans, and other country colours; the other on the grey side for blacks, greys, blues, and the more town tones.

Be sure the stockings you buy are big enough in the feet and long enough in the leg. The most unnerving sound is to bend down for something and hear a nylon thread go *ping* across your knee.

If you've become addicted to dark stockings or tights, be careful not to look like a Charles Addams heroine.

Brightly coloured leotards, stockings, and knee socks play an exciting role in leisure and at-home time. If you live in the suburbs or the country, hosiery fads such as these contribute much to your daytime hours as well.

If you've become addicted to dark stockings or tights, be careful not to look like a Charles Addams heroine. The 'beatnik' bit is wonderful for sloppy, slushy days, but should not be allowed to take over.

Most hosiery dries quickly, so don't send your husband howling from the display of inanimate legs in the bathroom. Try to wash your 'smalls' when he's not around, roll them in Turkish towels for about a half-hour. You'll find that another half-hour of drying will do the trick.

PETTICOATS

As you may know from my designs in the past, I am particularly partial to petticoats and have spent much time developing special fabrics for improving their contour, wearability, and 'careability'. Since fashion silhouettes change all the time, it's difficult to give hard and fast rules on full petticoats. Just be sure you wear the proper fullness under each dress.

Unlike slips, which are basic underwear and must be washed every day, petticoats are outer-wear and should be regarded as such in terms of selection and *care*. Build a petticoat wardrobe of varying silhouettes which can be worn separately or in combination to fit under full skirts of different designs. Some petticoats billow from the waist, some from below the hipbone. Never buy a petticoat without trying it on so that you can see where the fullness falls on your bone structure.

Since most designers of full-skirted fashions also design petticoats, try to match up your selections. Construction differs, so you might as well have the benefit of the same designer's thinking in both dress and petticoat. Regarding expense, a petticoat wardrobe changes gradually since full-skirt styles change gradually season by season. Soft petticoats are best because they take on the shape of the dress.

Colour range depends on how much of a petticoat girl you are. I have a red one to perk up printed cottons in summer, as well as a range of pastels plus white and black.

SLIPS

It is no exaggeration to say that you need a suitable slip for every dress you own, providing the right colour, fullness, and length underneath – at least a dozen half-slips and at least one white whole slip which you will find invaluable with sheer dresses, both slim and full. Be sure your slim hips are slim enough and short enough for reed-slim sheaths. White, pink, blue, beige, and black comprise a basic year-round slip wardrobe, with additional prints and colours for pampering purposes when the usual slip colours seem too dreary.

BOUDOIR WEAR

If you are a recent bride living off the spoils of a bridal shower, you probably have an abundance of sleep garments in every conceivable style and colour. Be certain each fits well before inclusion in your wardrobe. See that they flatter your figure and that the colours, which are generally pastel, go well with your natural skin tone, *without* make-up. Remember this is one time you can't rely on make-up for your shading. Your boudoir is like the countryside. It depends on nature's grooming.

I adore sleepwear, especially pyjamas, not only the practical 'little boy' styles, which are so crisp and comfortable to sleep in, but all the frillier styles besides. But, whether you prefer pyjamas or gowns – have at least six currently new ones in your active sleep wardrobe. Pay as much attention to their style and fit as you do your outer wear. The master bedroom is not a college dormitory or a camping trip up the Orinoco. It is a private retreat set apart from the outside world, even if it is furnished with such mechanical wonders as television suspended from the ceiling and an electric coffee pot that wakes you up, combs your hair, and spoon-feeds you at that first sip of liquid strength.

Think pretty when making your selections and, please, no safety pins. Replace buttons and ribbons almost before they need it. Fastidiousness is essential; make it a permanent part of your sleepwear.

Robes are another excess of mine. I don't believe in wearing one robe to death any more than I would wear one dress morning, noon, and night until it fell off my back. When I get home from the office each evening the first thing I do is kiss my son Taffy, the second is take off my dress and get into a robe, even before I decide on what to wear for the evening.

If my husband and I are going out, I bathe and get back into a robe, slipping into my dress at the last possible moment. If we're staying in, like as not we will have dinner in pyjamas and robes.

For purely psychological reasons, have at least one ultra-glamorous negligee to wear when you're not feeling well. You can feel like the heroine of a Victorian novel being pampered and loved and fed chocolate creams on a horsehair sofa. Also, have a lush bed jacket to brighten up forced confinement in bed.

Perhaps I'm a little oversensitive to the need for glamour in every phase of a wardrobe, but at the speed with which we all live, it's nice sometimes to drag your foot in a furry mule and slow things down a bit.

For the morning you need a warm, tailored robe, slim in cut and ankle-length. I think this length is best because short robes expose the unattractive sight of a rumpled nightie or pyjama bottoms – or bare white legs – protruding underneath.

A terry-cloth robe or wrap-around is a great item too. You'll find it really ultra-practical: the terry not only absorbs moisture but is a cosy cover-up that is not damaged by water or body lotions you may use after bathing.

I think here is a good place to mention shoulder cape-covers for make-up, although they are one step removed from the category of robes. At the time this book goes to press I am introducing a new design, a poncho-style make-up cape in a Dacron and cotton fabric, which is long enough for moving from one room to another when someone's around. There is a little pocket for sachets so that an aura of scent accompanies every movement.

European women are more feminine in their boudoir wear than Americans. I grew up hanging over a washbowl to put on my make-up. My mother uses a make-up table. I have tried it, but still can't get used to the idea of sitting down. I feel that I'm missing something when I return to my stance at the sink, but the poncho make-up cover makes up for some of this self-neglect.

Whosoever's design you wear, have a protective cover while you brush your hair or apply splashy lotions.

KITCHEN WEAR

A chronic blight on the American home scene is sleepwear in the kitchen! Negligees, bathrobes, and terry towels do *not* belong with food, pots, and pans. The kitchen is your natural setting as a woman and you should look beautiful, not bedraggled, in it. Whether you go to work or work at home – or both – take advantage of the opportunity the kitchen offers for expressing your wifely qualities in what you wear. Whatever the prevailing fashion outside your home, kitchen wear is timeless. Pinafores, organdies, and aprons look wonderful, as do gay cotton wrap-arounds that slip on over your dress while you make breakfast or wear instead of a dress at other times. Too much attention is paid to kitchen equipment and decor; too little to what is worn in this setting. Why look like Cinderella's crotchety stepmother when you can be a lyrical embodiment of all that a home and hearth means!

An apron wardrobe should range from frilly half-styles to an enormous butcher's apron that makes you beguilingly small by contrast.

SHOES

Because of climate and seasonal changes, I will approach a shoe wardrobe with a generalized viewpoint. Vacation and travel suggestions are covered elsewhere.

Have as many pairs of shoes as your wardrobe needs. Personally, I don't think it's extravagant to have lots of shoes. I hate pedantic footwear. I adore colour on the foot and think of red as a basic shoe. Somehow colour acts as a springboard, lifting you off the floor in a light step. A dress can't stand alone. It must be part of a composition and shoes are, facetiously speaking, the 'groundwork'. They should have vigour and identity, not merely keep your feet dry.

My one bugaboo is white shoes. Of all accessories, they are the most difficult. They really have to belong to a costume. If you haven't lots of white clothes, do without them. Don't automatically buy a pair of white kid to wear willy-nilly all summer. If you have an all-white costume and want an all-white look, choose a pair of shoes that match exactly. The single-tone harmony can be marred by off-shades of white accessories. White shoes with anything but a white costume somehow become 'bottom-heavy'.

To borrow an old saw, be sure the shoe fits. If it doesn't, be merciless. Give it away. The money you spend on its replacement would have gone to a chiropodist. The soft, glovelike fit of ballet slippers and casual footwear has seeped into more formal footwear. The dancer's mould not only is the best texture for your feet but generally keeps the shape of the last.

For evening wear I believe in having a rainbow collection of satin shoes in simple pump and sandal styles. They go with almost any after-five ensemble and, as explained in 'You Can't Go Home Again', page 19, satin shoes can transform a day dress into cocktail wear, turning day into night with a Cinderella slipper.

Satin shoes are classics and can be an active contribution to your wardrobe for years.

DRESSES AND SUITS

So much depends on where you live and how you spend your day, I won't presume to outline specific items you should or should not have. From my personal point of view as a working wife and mother, here are some of the elements I consider most important in a dress and suit wardrobe.

GOING TO WORK. To be well dressed during your working day away from home, comfort is a prime essential that cannot be stressed strongly enough. You must travel to your job; you must work efficiently all day. A neckline that strangles, a waistline that binds, a bodice that inhibits your breathing will do more to exhaust you, hamper your activity, and generally make you miserable than all the work crises imaginable.

Comfort does not mean sloppiness or ungainliness. Comfort does mean clothes that are cut to move with you. It means styling created for a body in action.

Going-to-work clothes need more attention than any other category. You wear them more than any other category, and often, when you don't go home to change for the evening, you wear them for fun as well.

Avoid extremes. You needn't be dowdy, ultra-conservative in choice of colour, or devoid of original styling. Express your personality as much as you can in colours, textures, and lines. On the other hand, let no hint of the boudoir or cocktail hour

We wives are emotional beings. Clothes play an important role in emotional control.

slip in. For instance, a black broadcloth suit with a black satin collar can go to work in the morning, but the big black satin stole you might normally wear with it is all wrong. If you need it for the evening, tuck it in your bag out of sight all day.

Another thing to avoid is the 'too-sporty' look often clung to by recent college graduates or wives who live in the country. If you need heavy woollen socks to get through the driveway to make your train, well and good; but that's where your tote-bag comes in handy to carry your change of shoes and hose. Whatever the weather, black socks and loafers are not meant for the office.

We wives are emotional beings. Clothes play an important role in emotional control. If you go to work knowing you look wonderful, feeling at ease, comfortable, and appropriately garbed, you're bound to be more alert and more able to cope with problems, including the unexpected. Getting the habit of dressing well every day will prevent panic at an unexpected situation at work, or *after* work for that matter.

As for suits, it all depends on whether or not you're a 'suit girl'. There's no rule that says you must wear them to work if you prefer them for country or evening wear. There's no rule to prevent your wearing them every day as part of a large suit wardrobe if they fulfil your fashion preference.

What I especially like about suits is that blouses can be so beautifully individual. What I especially don't like is the blouse that won't stay put in the skirt. There are several remedies for this problem. When I make a blouse, I always put in a waistline for definition that will stay secure. One of the great *couturières*, Sophie of Saks Fifth Avenue, has devised an elastic attachment which fastens to your stockings and holds the blouse down that way.

My models have tricks of their own. One sews tiny metal weights along the hem to anchor it down. Another tucks her blouse inside her girdle.

In choosing suit colours and fabrics, be careful of blacks and navies, which can be disastrous lint-catchers.

COCKTAILS AND EVENING WEAR. Seriously consider the long evening dress, a style which is slowly making a comeback and needs some impetus. If you say there is no occasion, *make* the occasion. Have a small party and request the guests to dress. One hostess can start a trend. Formal evening wear has

Satin shoes. Marvellous jewellery. White kid shorties. Festive handbag. These can transform a simple, uncluttered wool or silk into a gala ensemble.

a longer life than short cocktail wear. I think no wardrobe is complete without at least one long dress.

Cocktail wear can be made of any fabric and be of almost any style design and still be appropriate. I believe in accessories as the prime factor in cocktail garb. Satin shoes. Marvellous jewellery. White kid shorties. Festive handbag. These can transform a simple, uncluttered wool or silk into a gala ensemble.

Cocktail clothes may be bare if you have a good suntan and are feeling in the pink. They may be all covered up if your skin is winter-white or the least bit sallow, or if you have a cold or aren't feeling in top form.

The important thing in what you wear is mood, which may be expressed with colour, texture, or design – or a careful combination. Much depends on approach and personality. Because I'm always cold in the wintertime, I avoid bare styles and depend on covered-up wools and jerseys. A favourite cocktail costume consists of a sweater-knit dress in winter white with long, tight sleeves, worn with a silk chiffon at the collar and a simple diamond pin, rhinestone bracelet, and satin shoes. The soft white texture with accents of glitter are an expression of winter gaiety and in the meantime keep me snug as a bug.

SPORTSWEAR. This category overlaps dresses in that I believe dresses should be worn for most casual and spectator occasions. Slacks are not for tennis matches, race tracks, or ball parks; and blue jeans should stay in the old corral or come out only for square dancing, moonlight beach parties, or painting the back-yard furniture.

A recent bride I know had a lopsided bachelor-girl wardrobe that consisted of jeans, baggy skirts, some collegiate-looking wools for work, and about 28 cocktail dresses. Since her marriage, she's replaced her 'raunchy-looking cow pants' with 'the sweater look', a sportswear wardrobe of soft, pleated skirts, cashmere and wool slipovers, and classic shirtwaists.

The extent of your sportswear depends on your activities: whether you participate in club sports such as golf, whether you attend sporting events with your husband or children, whether you live in the country or city. If you were used to slouching around in jeans as a bachelor girl, it may take a bit of adjusting to dresses and skirts for your new role. It's been said marriage is a pretty big adjustment generally, and I believe dressing as a *wife*, not a schoolgirl, is as important as poaching eggs just so and getting your husband's suits pressed.

Speaking generally, have enduring sportswear that will serve you. A bulky tweed coat, a shaggy country suit if you live in the city, a collection of tweeds, wools, leathers, and cashmeres for the country or suburban life.

Dress properly for active sports. Wear a golf dress on the links, a tennis dress on the courts or, if you prefer, shorts and T-shirts; white is regulation for almost all courts. Not only does it look best but some courts won't permit you to play in anything else.

COATS. Where coats were once thought of as being for 'work', for 'dress up', or for travel, now there are more coats than ever to cover and enhance a wardrobe. With the new uses of fabrics, textures, and linings, coat 'thinking' has radically changed.

Linings add much to a coat wardrobe. While a particular lining may match one dress, it can enrich several others as well. For instance, a brown plaid lining gives new dimension to white or black or off-white or yellow or tones of brown or red or the tiniest speck of colour in the plaid.

Fur linings are my idea of luxury and the well-cared for feeling. A fur-lined tweed can go anywhere and keep you warm besides. Luxury tweeds with lush inside interest are representative of the new coat thinking that began with polo coats for over-the-shoulder wear with evening clothes – now a fixture of country-club dressing.

As a city gal, I have translated the polo-coat idea to a bright red plaid wool coat which serves a dual purpose in much the same way. In the broadest fashion sense, an extra-casual coat can double for formal occasions, whereas an in-between style cannot. As with the polo coat that goes to the country-club dance, my red plaid goes to the office, but I have also worn it for such gala occasions as New Year's Eve over a long red flannel evening gown and to a fancy ball over the shoulders of a white cut velvet gown with a red sash.

For evening, it's the texture interest that counts. The red plaid – or even a plain red coat – gave a feeling of soft plushness with the warmth and gaiety of red. Another effective combination of the formal and casual might be a satin coat over a tweed dress for cocktails, while an all-satin ensemble might be much too formal for such an occasion.

If yours is a limited coat wardrobe, your basic coat does not have to be that old stand-by, black. It can be red or grey or beige, although the latter admittedly needs more frequent cleaning. Textured and tweed coats are often more adaptable than smooth-surfaced styles and should be considered as a basic coat. If you know you're going to wear one coat a great deal, avoid black because it is difficult to keep free of lint and extremely difficult to match up with other blacks. Black ensembles are chic when they're perfectly co-ordinated; rather drab when they just miss.

At the other end of the spectrum is the white coat, which waned many years ago and is slowly returning as a fashion item. If you like white, think of it in terms of winter daytime wear over dark or bright colours.

The summer-coat idea has more or less given way to jackets, stoles, shrugs, and various evolutions of the cover-up. There is still room for pastel tweeds if a serious coat is needed, and a thin satin coat if a gala covering is in order for an air-cooled restaurant or theatre. Summer satin is particularly effective over a simple but elegant cotton.

As a seaside dweller in summer, I have depended on sweaters for everything from an early-morning walk to cocktails on a neighbour's boat. Jewelled and furred sweaters can be very gala for evening, but *be sure they're* not *overburdened. A* friend of mine had a sweater trimmed with an enormous fox collar that descended the front of the sweater almost to the waist. One day she removed the collar to have the sweater cleaned and discovered that the fur alone made a perfectly charming circlet that just fit over her shoulders as an ideal summer fur.

Extra jackets are an important adjunct to your coat wardrobe too. Choose them carefully to blend with your other clothes rather than because they're pretty in themselves. Fur jackets are great, as is short, colourful tweed. I like leather jackets for suburbia and the country more than for town – with a definite taboo on pastel leathers for city wear.

RAINCOATS

The rainwear picture has been a sunny one for the last few years, and the bad-weather forecast continues to be good. The one-raincoat wardrobe is a thing of the past. Now you can have a stormcoat with a fur or alpaca lining to get you through 'impossible' days, and fabulous rainproofed fabrics in a galaxy of styles suitable for the rain or even when it's only a dismal threat in the sky. Fur and velvet trims and unusual linings have made rainwear so beautiful that often a raincoat can overlap your regular coat collection.

For winter evenings – when it's certain to rain five minutes before you're embarking on dress-up party – there are wonderful water-resistant velvets in voluminous styles that will protect your pretty dress and cloak you in splendour besides.

You'll need an additional lightweight raincoat for summer. Winter weights would suffocate you. Don't depend on something innocuous to keep the sun-showers off.

Oilskin coats and fisherman hats add colour and swashbuckle to country wear. The buckles especially have an air of protectiveness, and the entire concept looks great with boots, which are a necessity in the country or at the seashore. Every woman looks marvellous in a slicker in the right setting – which is *not* the city! At the risk of being too arbitrary, I will certainly concede that a slicker is fine for city dog-walking or a trip to the launderette. But slickers are wrong for the office or any social setting beyond the primitive life facing the elements.

The most luxurious texture there is, fur casts a glow of softness on your complexion and increases your awareness of yourself as a woman. From a rabbit to chinchilla, real or frankly fake, furs should play an important part in your wardrobe.

Keep your fur thinking flexible and timely. Don't think you 'must have a mink stole' as a status symbol or proof of social station. A mink stole is to my mind a comfortable item, yet it is not, strictly speaking, a 'fashion' item because it is timeless rather than timely.

I adore the extravagant feeling of mink but prefer it in more flexible form than a stole. If you have an old stole that you continue to wear because of the initial investment, have it made into a luxurious muff or use it to line a tweed jacket. Give it a new life with a new, exciting treatment. Only one thing, please – keep it off the poodle!

While I don't think of the mink stole as all-important, it certainly has its place in a wardrobe.

The satin or velvet evening coat in a gay colour is a lively substitute that offers more cover-up protection. Many women think it the better part of valour to freeze on a cold night wrapped in a mink stole. I don't agree. A huge red velvet coat with a weatherproofed surface will cloak you in finery and stand up to cold blasts and those inevitable drizzles that always seem to fall when you're trying to find a taxi or walking to where the car is parked. Pastels lavishly trimmed with mink are another luxury fur fashion that couldn't be more flattering.

And while on the subject of flattery, I must put in a word for fur hats. Whether you're an up-to-date Theda Bara or have cold ears, a fur hat is one of the most glamorous accessories you can possess. If you have a fur coat, try to match the fur exactly with a hat or hood.

Fur coats fall into three categories: luxury, casual, frankly fake.

LUXURY FURS have improved vastly in recent years because of improved fashion techniques. Furs are now processed so that they can be cut and styled with the manoeuvrability of fabric. Combinations such as seal with mink and otter with mink have offered new fashion excitement. You can expect a luxury fur coat to have style and perfect fit in addition to beautiful skins.

CASUAL FURS are the raccoons, moleskins, and other inexpensive pelts which adapt so well to changing fashions. From year to year they appear as trimming or jackets or linings or in whatever new way a designer may try and the public may accept.

FAKE FURS should be regarded as a separate fashion entity, not as a substitute for real fur. Being frankly fake, they are really a new luxurious fabric which add immeasurably to a wardrobe. They are only effective when worn boldly at face value, never when hopefully masquerading as something else.

Remember that furs are a state of mind, a symbol of affection and a mirror of luxury and femininity. I doubt if even diamonds can compare with the mood furs create. Keep your choice of furs and their uses extremely personal to satisfy your own caprices. As an example, I am enamoured of fur bags, and have several in sizes ranging from a tiny clutch to a huge tote. Because of the pleasure I get from carrying a fur bag, I even use the smallest ones in summer with my cottons for a bit of

Don't buy nondescript millinery. Make every hat tell a story, fit an ensemble, fill a fashion need.

unusual chic that works out very well. Furs are special and personal. They require your special and personal attention.

HEADWEAR

Besides making you pretty, hats should be functional. In winter they should keep your ears warm. In summer they should shade your eyes. Whatever the style, they should fit securely and flatter your face from every angle.

Many women virtually ignore hats in their wardrobes, a tendency to be mourned. Historically and romantically, hats have been a symbol of a woman, yet today men wear more hats than women – which is a deplorable situation.

Don't shun hats. They are a difficult part of the wardrobe, but worth perfecting. The cliche about a woman buying a hat to cheer her up couldn't be truer. A hat can buoy your emotions as well as your looks. Since every wardrobe must have basic headwear for church, community affairs, and extremes of cold and hot weather, don't take the first hat that comes along or the least conspicuous one as a 'necessary evil'. Develop your own hat stylishness as a means of expressing your individualism.

What I don't like are sneaky little hats that perch on the head indecisively. If you're going to wear them, make them important. A red fox beret. A helmet of daisies. A huge straw skimmer. Don't buy nondescript millinery. Make every hat tell a story, fit an ensemble, fill a fashion need.

In addition, you'll need a hood style for automobile journeys, protective headgear for spectator sports out in the open, and a collection of straws and piqués in summer to cover your head and cast pretty shadows on your face.

As mentioned under FURS, if you have a fur coat, have a hat or hood in matching skins. I don't think fur coats look quite right with flowered or straw hats. Fur should be accompanied by fur – or an important-looking fur felt that gives the same texture feeling. A fur coat should be balanced with weight on the head. Otherwise with an enormous fur coat you risk looking like a pinhead, having a slight misproportion between head and body. There is nothing more romantic than a huge Anna Karenina fur toque or a full, cavernous fur hood that evokes a spirit of adventure – and is never out of fashion.

Classic styles make the best basic-hat wardrobe because they are easiest to wear for most women – which probably explains why they have become classics. Two leading examples are the cloche and beret. Depending on fabric, both are suitable for country and city. Berets are not quite so practical as the cloche when it comes to holding your hair down, but they look well – which proves how far the Basque peasant garb has come in the fashion world.

Head scarves have replaced hats in a good deal of suburban wear, which is okay if you know how to wear a head scarf so that it is flattering and co-ordinated with your outfit. But scarves can slip and be uncomfortable after a while. When I'm living the country life on Long Island during the summer, I find hats more comfortable and more fun. Straws, *piqués*, cotton fabrics stay put on my head without strangling me and shade my eyes, which a scarf can't do.

If you travel at all, it's important to have one packable hat. It might be a beret or a soft-brim model specifically designed to fold up or roll up for packing. If you haven't one and will be visiting churches, it's very romantic to wear a very pretty starched lace handkerchief on top of your head. Mantillas are nice too, but you must know how to wear them. Avoid the tourist mistake of a black lacy mantilla over a cotton dress.

Recently when a friend of mine was married, I designed the clothes for the bridal party. Her headpiece was a dramatic affair that swept back from her face and floated to the floor behind her. In contrast, each of the bridesmaids wore the small stiffened lace handkerchiefs set squarely atop their heads.

Since your face is what most people see first, your hat should be both flattering and timely. Because the calendar says it's spring, wait until the snow melts and the greenery begins to appear before putting on a hatful of daffodils which to me is just as inappropriate as wearing an organdie dress and open-toed sandals for a snowball fight.

GLOVES

I've always thought it was impossible to have too many gloves, but recently I changed my mind. You *can* have too many gloves if they create confusion and waste time when you're fishing for the right pair. If your gloves are in a sad state, go through them, weed out the unwearables, pair up scattered mates. Keep colours together.

Most important in a glove wardrobe is white – shorties in cotton and kid, longer lengths as needed for style preference and formality. For every formal occasion where gloves extend up over the elbows, I prefer skin tones to white. One of my favourite examples is an embroidered black velvet ball gown which I tried first with white then with black gloves, neither of which were right. A pair of long, long tan kid gloves created exactly the right illusion.

However, I have gone on record for posterity in a pair of long white gloves in the Philadelphia Museum where a figure of me stands besides the most famous of all white glove girls, Princess Grace of Monaco. My reason for being there is that I won an award for Twentieth Century Design and was asked to present the Museum with the gown I wore for my acceptance. It's a gold embroidered lace ball gown completely strapless, ankle length, and stiffly crinolined, with a formal headdress, a white fox muff, and the long white gloves.

I have only one tiny regret. The Museum sent people to take my measurements to make a dummy, and when I arrived at the Museum with the gown before the dedication, I was both flattered and dismayed. The face is absolutely beautiful, but I couldn't zip up the dress. Being proud of a narrow rib cage and an 18-inch waist-line, I am hoping that one day they will pare down the figure to its rightful proportions.

For day-to-day wear, I prefer white cotton shorties to everything else, and I always carry at least one extra clean pair. In this respect, I consider white shorties as I do my stockings: they must be washed after every wearing and it's good to have a large supply ready to be worn.

For sportswear, oatmeal and brown pigskins will augment any ensemble, and don't forget a pair of very warm gloves for below-freezing days. One of the less attractive sights is a woman blowing on her frozen fingers.

The only time I don't wear white cotton gloves is at the height of winter – with the exception of white strings with tweeds. During the very cold weather I choose between leather or suede and wool jersey. Eight-button black kids are sombre but solid and warm in winter. Shades of beige in leather and suede are wonderful, but be careful of matching problems with both since these are difficult to match exactly. If you like beige tones, build up a separate glove wardrobe of tan tones to be always sure of co-ordination. Gold jersey gloves are basic because they can be worn with almost any colour scheme. Various shades of yellow offer much the same benefits.

Odd colours are good if you can afford them or if you're glove-mad. Otherwise you can safely rely on beige and white and an occasional black.

Gloves and shoes need not match. In fact, I prefer them not to. If the shoes are an unusual colour, white or neutral gloves are best.

From this basis, you're on your own in the fabulous jungle of colours, leathers, fabrics, and lengths. All I can say in this limitless area is: Don't buy a strange new design or an out-of-this-world colour 'just because'. Know why and how you will wear unusual gloves before you buy them.

HANDBAGS

Besides the all-important tote-bag in either a neutral colour or black flexible leather or weave, build a cohesive handbag group. Along with shoes, handbags have the longest fashion span. They don't go out of style so readily and are adaptable to many costumes and moods.

In addition to the cavernous tote, your suit and coat bags should also be quite large, regardless of your height and weight. Nothing bores me more than this nonsense about small women having to go through life with pintsized handbags – and vice-versa, the tall girls who sincerely believe they can never be seen with a small clutch bag.

The size of your bag should be governed by the size and weight of your costume and its function. A small, ineffectual bag with heavy tweeds is just silly. You need a large rugged handbag to round off the ensemble. With handbags it's the costume dimension rather than the personal dimension that counts.

Other than suit and coat bags, I prefer to have lots of small bags in various colours and fabrics which I can carry inside my tote if necessary. For daytime, calf, suede, and patterns to match your shoes; for evening, brocaded, satin, and velvet clutch bags to accent or match an ensemble. In addition, a smallish fur bag which can be the one luxury accent with a day or evening costume all year round.

To me, small bags epitomize mobility. They are big enough

For the strictly 'fun' side of your handbag wardrobe, choose a fashion item with excitement and immediacy.

to carry personal 'necessaries'. Everything else goes into the tote-bag, which can then be left in the car, the office, or checked somewhere while you conduct the business at hand unencumbered. My objection to larger handbags as such is that they get terribly heavy and cannot be temporarily abandoned or easily manoeuvred in restaurants and theatres.

For summer, trade in your leather tote for a straw or wicker carry-all with, if possible, a matching small straw bag inside. Straw is the best texture for summer. I don't like white bags. White leather at its best is difficult to keep once you've unwrapped it. White plastic looks like oilcloth. White fabrics need glazing and then they look like plastic, which looks like oilcloth. The idea of the white summer handbag to go with everything is not only unfashionable but impractical, since it means walking around most of the summer with a sullied accessory.

In addition to straw, black patent is good for a summer tote, although oddly enough it may look too heavy in a small clutch bag. Other effective summer bags are large print fabrics and tapestry totes – as long as the textures and colours blend with what you're wearing.

Aside from my feelings about white summer bags, there are two more protests which in all fashion conscience I must make here. One is the bag heavily encrusted with flowers, jewels, buttons, bows, poodles, and perhaps a replica of Sherwood Forest, which detracts rather than adds to an ensemble. The other is transparent bags, which look like something medicinal that must be on view at all times in case it should explode. Even at their most meticulous (which is rare), crystal-clear bags are purely show-off, and I wouldn't blame any pickpocket for going after booty so wantonly displayed. I suppose this feeling stems from my childhood when, if anything was stolen from me, my mother would say that it was my fault because obviously I had carelessly tempted the thief to rob me.

For the strictly 'fun' side of your handbag wardrobe, choose a fashion item with excitement and immediacy. At this writing, it might be something in fur, such as a scaled-down suitcase in zebra or leopard. Fun fashions are not staples and should be considered an addition, not a substitution.

Think of your handbag in terms of a collection, filling in colours and fabrics as needed, experimenting with new combinations to vary the look of your total wardrobe. As a final word, don't let them get shoddy. Your small bags especially are what people see first, so give them the attention you give your other niceties.

PERFUME

I believe in the One-Scent Stamp, that is, the one hint of an aroma that automatically means you, but not as a result of using one perfume only. The One-Scent Stamp is the personalized composite of the different perfumes you use plus the lotions and cosmetics that comprise your daily beauty ritual. If you're wise enough to have picked out a husband, you should by now have narrowed your choice of perfumes to a degree of recognition so that your coat, your scarf, your handkerchief are recognizably 'yours' to anyone who picks them up. It's perhaps the same principle as giving your dog a pair of your socks to comfort him when he's going to be by himself and lonely.

Quantitatively speaking, your scent supply depends on your personal tastes and what you've received as gifts. I've often thought that if there was one inclination I would like to indulge someday, all caution to the winds, it would be perfume. I love being surrounded by beautiful bottles of intoxicating fragrances. The more I have, the more luxurious and pampered I feel. The only analogy I can think of in a man's life is pipes. Some men have 40 or 50 in various textures and shapes. They couldn't possibly smoke them all at once, any more than I could use all my perfume at once – but they're nice to contemplate all the same.

However many bottles you have, only open one or two at a time. Perfume seems to disappear into thin air while you're looking at it.

Beyond the borders of your dressing table, use sachet bags or powder to infuse your clothes with fragrance. As an added note: atomizers prolong the life of scents and increase their effectiveness.

SCARVES

I believe in scarves – I must have about two hundred of them. They are my pet accessory because they can be worn with such singularity. I rarely go out – or stay home for that matter

When you see a bewitching
scarf, don't resist.
Buy it on the spot because
it may be gone the next time
you shop.

– without one of some size, shape, or fabric around my neck or tucked in my jacket.

Scarves are fun and not too expensive. They are the one category you can build on 'impulse buying'. When you see a bewitching scarf, don't resist. Buy it on the spot because it may be gone the next time you shop.

Your scarf wardrobe can be built steadily because scarves are timeless. The only weeding out that's necessary is to eliminate shabby or spotted members. Include chiffons, satins, challis, silks, ribbon, fur, lamé, leather, *piqué*, or mesh. Choose stripes, prints, checks, solids, Paisleys. Long. Short. Square. Tiny neckpiece scarves to insert in the neckline of a sweater or dress. Enormous chiffons for swathing the neck and shoulders inside a satin theatre coat. Scarves are indefatigable, and if you can't find exactly what you want for a certain costume, you can always make your own.

It's fun to fill in a scarf collection and not too expensive. You can spend $1.50 or $150 for one of the fabulous gold woven Indian scarves. Wonderful effects can be had for next-to-nothing or by spending the proverbial fortune whichever is your heart's desire.

Always experiment to achieve new results. Last year, by accident, I found that I had one 'key' scarf which did wonderful things for almost my entire wardrobe, fitting in with everything I owned. It's a mustardy gold and I wore it with red, with black, with green tweeds – with everything. The texture of the scarf has remarkable qualities which enable it to 'take on' many tones, including to my surprise the metallic hue of a bronze ribbon in my hair.

Scarves can contribute to a single-colour theme for a segment of unity in your wardrobe for a season. The single-colour theme is worth looking into and interesting to try. The GREEN LOOK or BLACK LOOK or BEIGE LOOK are most effective – the beige, for instance, going from deep brown to almost white in merging shades of tan.

UNDERWEAR

Underpinnings have two functions: utility and glamour. I believe in girdles or elasticized panties for everything, including shorts. Figure control at all times improves posture and stops you from spreading. The idea of not wearing a girdle under a full skirt is wrong. As for slim, tight skirts, I think there should be a federal law against wearing them girdleless. My mother put me into a girdle when I was 13; I have worn one ever since.

Have enough foundations for active sports, at-home clothes, and evening wear, including one with a loop for attaching a backless bra. Girdles last longer when nourished by rest. Never wear the same girdle two days in a row. And please, no safety pins. Repair garters at once. Safety pins tear the fabric, leave rust spots when washed, and are hazardous to your skin.

Bras probably need more replenishing than any other underwear item. However firm their original construction, constant washing must take its toll. Even if the rubber or straps do not yet show signs of wear, they will, to coin a phrase, lose 'their hold' with time. Be certain you have the right bra contour for every dress and silhouette. And again – no safety pins. Wash bras after each wearing; most are made of miracle fabrics and dry in a matter of hours.

Continually add new foundations, both girdles and bras, so that you always have something fresh and alert to put on when a worn garment begins to fail.

The soundest approach to a basic wife-dressing wardrobe is to have the essential ingredients and blend carefully. It's a little bit like baking your first cake. Be confident, but be careful too.

❄ ❄ ❄

FIVE

The Care and Feeding of Your Wardrobe

A WORD TO HUSBANDS: *Dresses are like political opinions. There's always a newer, more exciting idea on the horizon, especially when conflicting parties are involved.*

Queen Anne Boleyn arouses little twinges of envy in me because I read somewhere that she wore her gowns once and tossed them to some waiting lady-in-waiting. When I mentioned this enchanting fact to my husband late one night when I was feeling too sleepy to hang up my dress, his only remark was, 'That's why Henry the Eighth had her killed'.

While men today aren't quite so forceful as Elizabeth I's father, there are plenty of other good reasons for taking care of your clothes so that you can wear them many times over with continuing enjoyment.

Clothes should be thought of individually in their care as well as their wear. Some fabrics need air, some dresses keep their shape better lying down, some sweaters should be popped into the refrigerator overnight. Some fabrics fade, some droop, some thrive in plastic bags.

GOING FROM HEAD TO TOE

HATS with brims must be kept on hat stands to keep their shape. To store a summer leghorn, stuff the crown with tissue paper and put the hat upside down into a hat box larger than the brim. Hats should be kept separate from each other, preferably in plastic hat boxes or ones with plastic windows so you can see inside. If some are in solid hat boxes, paste on a label to identify the contents, neatly printing RED VELVET CLOCHE, etc., so you won t have to drag out every box to find what you want.

Keep felt and velvet hats fresh with a hat brush or by wiping gently with the Scotch tape knuckle-duster that is so effective for brushing any article of clothing.

Crushable hats such as berets, knitted caps, and hoods may be kept together. They tend to get jumbled on a shelf, so keep them in a large box or stacked in a drawer.

SCARVES should be stored in a wide, shallow drawer rather than a deep one. They will be easier to go through this way. Separate scarves into categories, evening scarves on one side, sportswear on the other, or into colour groups.

Whenever you're ironing, make it a habit to check through your collection for any that need a quick freshener. Otherwise, you would rarely bother to heat up the iron for just one little scarf. In the actual ironing, be sure to have the right temperature and be careful not to iron in folds. Press the scarf flat out and then fold gently so as not to make creases.

If you have several heavy winter scarves or shawls, you may want to hang them on a hanger in your cupboard, slipped over the bar of a wooden hanger or clamped into a skirt hanger. If they're made of slippery material that may be marred by a clamp hanger, drape them around a quilted hanger and fasten with clips.

BLOUSES behave best on hangers. Ideally, have one section of your cupboard divided vertically with a low rod for skirts and an upper rod for blouses. White and light-coloured blouses should be protected by plastic bags or at least shoulder covers. Sleeveless and slippery blouses require foam-rubber hangers (or hanger covers), which adhere to the fabric and don't let it fall to the floor.

Exceptions to the hanger rule are man-tailored shirts, which may be sent to the laundry with your husband's shirts and kept on shelves, cardboard and all, until needed; also wool or jersey blouses which may be folded like sweaters and kept with your knits in a deep drawer.

SWEATERS may be housed in plastic bags on shelves or in drawers. You can see that I think plastic bags are the greatest thing since '7-UP.' With plastic coverings, dust can't get in and you can see the sweaters clearly and handle them hurriedly without worrying about snags from your rings or other damage. Plastic bags help retain shape too, keeping the fibres compressed so they spring out when released. Your sweaters will be ready to travel too, since they can be shoved into a suitcase in their accustomed plastic container without a worry about getting them dirty.

Angora and other fluffy knits can be perked up with an overnight stay in the refrigerator – inside a plastic bag, of course. When you put them on, you'll be 'real cool' in more than the jazz sense.

Specific sweater care depends on the yarn. There are some miracle weaves you can toss into the washing machine and have them emerge in perfect shape. If you buy a miracle knit, keep the tag and read it carefully for washing instructions. For cashmeres and fine wools there are many excellent sweater soaps on the market, if you enjoy washing your own. To me, washing sweaters is like having a green thumb for gardening. Either you have the knack or you haven't. I haven't, and send mine to the cleaner's, which either washes or dry-cleans them, depending on colour. Whichever you do, be sure it's before the sweaters are so grimy that it's impossible to get them clean. Don't put away a dirty sweater, thinking you'll get around to it in time. The longer dirt has a chance to settle in, the harder it is to get out.

SKIRTS fare best on clamp-style skirt hangers – and only *one* to a hanger. Two or more is hazardous because too much pressure may injure the waistbands; too little because the increased bulk may send them all in a heap on the floor. For suits, get the combination hangers on which you can clamp the skirt inside the jacket. Notions departments constantly come up with new skirt-hanger designs. Take your pick, but be sure the clamping mechanism is well covered so that it doesn't dig into the fabric.

SLACKS AND SHORTS may be hung on skirt hangers. Or, shorts may be kept on shelves or in drawers, while cotton slacks will survive being slung over the rods of wooden hangers.

Get into the habit of brushing skirts after each wearing. It will cut down your cleaning bills and prolong the life of the fabric. Check hooks and eyes and snaps for prompt replacement. When they come off, the stress of your body movement on the fabric can distort its shape and make for shabbiness.

When it comes to DRESSES, I know I would stand to get a Congressional medal if I could figure out how to have enough cupboard space. All I can do is make some valiant suggestions for getting the most out of existing facilities.

First of all, throw away all those wire hangers. They are meant as carriers between the dry cleaner's and your home. They are not designed for long-time use, since clothes must be supported by heavier hangers to hold their shape.

Pastel wools and silks should be kept in simple zippered garment bags so they won't fade from the rays of the cupboard light. Black jersey requires a shoulder cover to keep away lint.

Bare-top dresses hang best when the bodice is folded inside-out over the skirt. If there are no loops on the inside waistband, make a few from the seam binding or some ribbon and sew them on. Clamp the waistband on a skirt hanger and sling the loops around the hanger neck for additional support, especially with heavy fabrics.

When wide skirts are cut on the bias and if they hang in one position for a long time without moving, they tend to droop unevenly. I have no magic answer for this problem except to suggest stretching out the undrooped parts by hand.

Since most fabrics need air, I've made it a habit to hang what I've just taken off on the shower rod in the bathroom. The moisture from my bath revives the fabric and takes out the wrinkles. If that's inconvenient, try hanging clothes at the front of your cupboard or outside your cupboard door overnight before returning them to their place among the other garments.

The wrong hanger can do almost as much harm to a dress as moths. The wrong shape or thickness can distort the lines and pull the fabric. There are many hangers from which to choose – colourful plastics that clean easily, quilted fabrics that are lovely but don't clean quite so easily, polished woods that go on for ever – but be sure wooden hangers are polished; otherwise they splinter and snag fabrics.

Uniformity of hangers gives your wardrobe cohesion. It's good for your morale to open your cupboard door and see everything looking nice. Plastic bags, boxes, and shoulder covers will protect your clothes, yet keep them visible.

Sachets in your cupboard are an excellent idea. Their scent will permeate your dresses and give you that well-cared-for feeling every time you get dressed.

COATS as well as other outdoor clothes should be kept in separate cupboards. Coats especially need big, strong hangers to keep the shoulders aligned. Never hang a damp coat in with others. It may spread the dampness and leave a musty smell generally. Hang wet clothes where air circulates freely, but not near direct heat. When dry, brush well before putting away.

With FURS, stoles are the big problem. There are wonderful new stole hangers in department stores which I'm sure are available all over. If you haven't seen one, it looks like a trapeze with a thick velvet rod suspended by chains from a hanger wide enough to hold wide stoles without crushing the fur. Never keep furs in boxes between wearings. They, too, need air. Keep white furs clean with individual covers made of porous fabric.

Shake furs vigorously each time you put them on and take them off. If you've been caught in the rain, let them dry away from heat before brushing them gently with a fur brush.

Expensive furs such as mink, sable, and sheared beaver should be professionally cleaned and glazed. Store winter furs during summer. Otherwise, don't worry about year-round furs, for pelts are not attacked by moths when in constant use.

For fake-fur care, read the tags carefully when you buy them and follow the advice recommended by the manufacturer. Care varies with content. Some of the fun furs can even be washed by machine!

UNDERWEAR, the often-neglected member of the wardrobe, is often jammed into an overstuffed drawer with little organization. I know. I'm the worst offender. Recently, however, I've found a way to overcome the jumble to some extent: by keeping all the items separate. That is – panties, girdles, bras, and slips in separate satin cases lined with sachet. Or, you might prefer to separate by colours, putting all your black underwear together in one case or drawer, whites and pastels in another. With either of these methods you'll be able to fish out the day's supply with a minimum of frenzy – and no wild tangle to straighten out later.

Keep underthings in good repair – slip straps, lace trims, elastics. This is one area where a stitch in time saves 'thine' underwear.

Hosiery boxes or cases are a good idea because they compress storage and tell you at a glance how many pairs you have. Also, they make a compact unit for packing or keeping separate from other things in a drawer.

Stocking care should begin when they're new. Wash them before the first wearing to assure elasticity and prevent the runs that sometimes pop in new hose. Wash stockings between each wearing with mild soap or one of the special hosiery suds that strengthen nylon threads. If you seem to be popping runs in exactly the same place all the time, check your garters to see if they have rough edges or try buying a larger or longer stocking than usual. You may be 'hard on stockings' because they're too small or short.

GLOVES should be stored flat, not rolled up or folded away except for long formal gloves, which may be folded in half if *absolutely* necessary; but they, too, are best kept flat. With leather gloves, always pull the fingers before putting them away. When you're ready to wear them again, they will spring into shape, hugging your fingers.

Dry washable leathers on frames, slipping them off the frames and on to your hands just before they're really dry. Cotton gloves you may dry flat and then give them a 'new' look by ironing the fingers. Glove washing is successful with just a little extra effort. You can't expect them to snap back into shape by themselves. They need a little hand-loving care.

If you are a glove loser, try stamping your name inside so that the finder can return them. If you are a *single-glove* loser, keep the left-over glove at least six months before discarding. Often a lost singleton turns up in a pocket — yours, your husband's, or the car!

A chronic glove-dropping friend of mine has taken to buying several pairs of the same style white gloves. In this way, when she loses one, she can save the other for matching up. This is a good idea for other classic glove styles in colours you wear all the time.

HANDBAGS may be lined up on shelves or stored in a deep drawer. Light-coloured leathers and fabrics should be protected from rubbing against each other and form dust particles in the air by plastic bags. If you have the cupboard space, dark bags with handles may be hung on special bag hangers. Small clutch bags may be stacked in drawers alongside gloves or scarves. Perishable evening bags stay fresh longer in plastic folders or wrapped in tissue paper between usings – especially gold, silver, and pale brocades, which lose their lustre quickly.

Keep your good leathers smooth and supple with saddle soap or neutral polish. If you have a large all-weather leather, it's a good idea to have it simonized for long wear.

BAUBLES, too, must breathe. Crushed together, they lose their vigour. Their lustre fades or is scratched. With the profusion and size of costume jewellery today, the ordinary jewel box may not be adequate. A neighbour of ours uses an old-fashioned sewing box that has an enormous plush-lined section which she uses for chunky bracelets and necklaces, and a dozen drawers formerly holding spools of thread now contain beads, earrings, and pins.

Another possibility is to use one or two deep drawers of a narrow chest or one large dresser drawer with section dividers. Real jewellery should be kept separate, each piece in an individual case or section of a plush-lined case and preferably under lock and key. Somehow there's a feeling of preciousness and security in having a safeguard.

By the way, I can advise you from gloomy experience not to hide valuables of any kind under a pile of slips or other lingerie. After our apartment was burgled several years ago – including my secret cache under my slips – the detectives told me that's where burglars look first because it's a very feminine hiding place.

BELTS are a bore, a bother, and a delight I wouldn't part with for a minute. I have tried everything. Belt hangers. Belt hooks. Special drawer. Special shelf. All that happens is every time I want a belt, I have to search for it.

Keep the belts that belong with certain dresses *with* certain dresses, not separately. This alone will considerably cut down the profusion of unmanageable belts that seem to multiply while you watch them.

Hang the matching belt on the hanger on which the dress is hung – not through the loops on the sides of the dress. In fact, these loops should be snipped off after you've bought the dress. Loops are put on by the manufacturers only to keep the belts attached for shipping purposes. They are *not* meant to be worn, and can detract from an otherwise perfect silhouette by billowing out.

The best way to solve the cumulative-belt problem is a cold examination of your collection. It's hard to do but discard those that are worn out. A partially frayed belt spreads shabbiness to a costume like a bad apple in a barrel.

Keep sports belts separate from daytime wear and these apart

from any you use for evening. Then you might try a technique I've heard about but haven't tried yet. It consists of driving a series of cup hooks into a wooden hanger and suspending one belt from each hook so that you don't have to take off a whole handful of belts to get at the one you want. Hooks go on both sides of as many hangers as are needed. It sounds like a good idea, because you can flip through until your choice comes to hand.

Of course if you're not up to doing it yourself, there are many commercial 'doo-dads' and new ones coming along every day, one of which may do the trick.

SHOES are my favourite accessory and I believe in giving them plenty of care and feeding because they add so much to my wardrobe. To get the most from your shoes, keep them covered, shaped, and repaired. Some women use individual transparent plastic bags for each pair. Others keep the original shoes boxes with a label pasted on each, indicating what's inside. At least your dressing room won't look like a shoe sale while you try desperately to find those blue silk sandals. Another sound idea, although somewhat in the Shangri-la class, is a separate shoe cupboard, very much like a bookcase with a door, where shoes are stored on ridged slanting shelves.

Keep your shoes clean and in repair. The minute a heel is scruffy, have it fixed. Don't wait until two minutes before you want to wear them before thinking of repairs. Your own supply of shoe polishes and brushes will keep your coloured shoes as well as traditional dark ones looking tiptop. Aim for up-to-the-minute wearability by brushing shoes before putting them away. Dirt won't have a chance to make a permanent impression.

With leather shoes, I've discovered one rather unorthodox quick-grooming technique that has its place in emergencies. If your shoes are a bit dull and drab and there's no handy shoeshine man, find a secluded corner, slip off one shoe, and briskly buff the other with the sole of your stockinged foot. It brings up a wonderful gloss and works well on husband's shoes too!

As for the general care and feeding of your wardrobe, try to keep the floors of your cupboards free of dust. Dust rises. Dust clings. Dust is the enemy. If the shortage of storage space that plagues us all forces you to keep things on the floor, see that

A healthy respect for your clothes shows an even healthier respect for your body and yourself as a person and a wife.

they are pulled out at least once a week and dusted when the cupboard floor is mopped or vacuumed.

I have not gone into the matter of lining drawers, preparing shelves, and other decor elements of housing your wardrobe since I feel these are part of home furnishing rather than wife-dressing. Do keep in mind that whatever adds to the cheeriness and cleanliness of your home is certainly beneficial to your clothes and the way they look.

A healthy respect for your clothes shows an even healthier respect for your body and yourself as a person and a wife. Your husband may tease you about 'Care and Feeding', but you may be sure his teasing will be tempered with pride.

❦ ❦ ❦

SIX

The Two-Faced Goddess: Taste and Money

'A modest woman dressed out in all her finery is the most tremendous object of the whole creation'

A WORD TO HUSBANDS: *'A modest woman dressed out in all her finery is the most tremendous object of the whole creation.'*

OLIVER GOLDSMITH

Fashion is a two-faced goddess who smiles with favour on judicious employment of *Taste* and *Money*. She must be approached seriously as well as light-heartedly on both counts. This is one goddess who has a flair for fun.

Good taste and the amount of money spent are interrelated but not necessarily dependent on each other. Expense does not assure good taste, nor is 'good' taste necessarily expensive to acquire. It's an accepted fact in the fashion world that many of America's best-dressed women do not have the most expensive wardrobes – and that some of America's worst-dressed women are those who spend thousands on clothes that couldn't be more wrong. So never delude yourself into being the poor little match girl with your nose pressed sadly against an out-of-reach price tag whimpering that life would be beautiful – if you only had the money.

A clothes budget is like Einstein's theory. It's based on relativity. The relative value of perhaps one very expensive coat against two less costly; of one good fur against a couple of fake furs; of an extreme high-fashion item against a classic.

The sole arbiter of what you wear is your own judgment. Price tags may limit your horizon. Labels may help you recognize designers whose styling has pleased you before. Saleswomen will advise you on what is most becoming. But the breathless words, 'I'll take this one', are your responsibility alone.

Good taste is harder to define than it is to recognize. It is an expression of personal style in terms of your physical proportions, your personality, and your way of life. It is an understanding of what is appropriate for a given set of circumstances. There are very few 'bad' clothes being made. What is 'bad' is clothes worn at the wrong time or place and in unsuitable combinations.

Furs are the perfect example of balancing taste with money. Decide how much money you can spend on them and how long they must last to justify the expense. Once the amount is settled, have a thoughtful session of self analysis. Would you be happy with one good fur? Can your budget cover the kind you want? Buying a ranch mink at the expense of the rest of your wardrobe becomes a foolish extravagance. Not having a mink coat is hardly a tragedy. Have it in other ways – and may I inject here the thought that mink should be the best possible quality even if that means a smaller quantity. There's nothing rattier-looking than poor pelts. For the luxury feeling of mink, have a huge muff or a jacket or a stole or – and this is my favourite – have a lavish mink lining for a coat or jacket which provides a gleaming fur backdrop for you when you toss it back from your shoulders.

Serious furs requires a sizable investment. Don't count on wearing them for years. Styles change and so does your fashion viewpoint. Less expensive and of equal, if different, taste are the fun furs and fake furs. Raccoon, rabbit, and moleskin – and their brother skins – have been appearing in exciting bags, hats, lap robes as well as conventional coats and jackets.

The only precious fur in my wardrobe is a Breath of Spring coat made of mink sides which cost about $1,000. While the cat has nine lives, the ever-so-much-more glamorous mink has many lives too, I discovered when exploring the possibility of a coat. The best mink coats are made of the backs of minks, while 'mink bellies' make up the bulk of mink linings for both men's and women's coats. The tails are used for trimmings and the throat or 'gill', which has a harlequin-patterned texture, finds its way into many fashion items – including an enormous mink gill tote given me by my husband.

The mink sides are what fascinate me. The little pieces are sewn together and cut as material, not worked as skin which permits more style leeway. If I could afford a magnificent ranch mink I would buy one; but it's not that important to the type of life we lead and I don't see how it could give me a more luxurious feeling than what I call my 'Mink Sides Masterpiece'.

Coats play an extravagant role in my wardrobe. I have many coats and prefer to put my money into various coats to make ensembles instead of one to go over everything.

Fur-trimmed sweaters are important fashion at this writing and probably will continue as such, with seasonal variations of style.

Diamonds can be vulgar if improperly worn — although that kind of vulgarity has a style of its own.

Fake furs are actually a 'category' of fabric which may be used *instead of* fur but not in imitation of it. Frankly fake furs are preferable to cheap-quality pelts and have a refreshing ingenuousness which candidly states that they are what they are and no fooling around.

When you think of furs, concentrate on the colour, the texture, and what these will do for your skin and eyes and hair. Whatever the fur and whether it's a small fox collar or a floor-length chinchilla, fur is the most flattering part of your wardrobe, and a place can be found for it in every budget.

Jewellery is another topic of taste. Diamonds can be vulgar if improperly worn – although that kind of vulgarity has a style of its own.

There are three categories of jewellery: *Real jewellery,* which includes precious stones and solid precious metals. *Imitation jewellery,* which copies the settings and workmanship in semi-precious stones, filled or plated metals, and other synthetic means. *Costume jewellery,* which is in a completely different category and is purely a fashion accessory which changes in style along with other fashion trends. It's important to realize that real and imitation jewellery are interchangeable in meaning and may be combined. Costume jewellery may properly take the place of neither.

Real and imitation jewellery are serious fashion; costume jewellery is not meant to be anything but fun. If a piece of costume jewellery becomes an integral part of your wardrobe, think seriously of having it copied in precious or semi-precious materials. This is rare because most costume jewellery goes in cycles or fads, such as the hoop earrings I introduced a few years ago. But sometimes you will adopt something, such as an unusual and inexpensive bangle that I've been wearing daily since the day I received it several months ago. If I don't tire of it, I will look into the cost of adding it to my permanent collection in an enduring metal.

A big question of taste and money is whether to concentrate on having a few 'good' pieces of jewellery or go all-out on costume designs.

My own approach is to do both simultaneously – at whatever speed is possible. Beginning with your engagement ring and wedding band, I think the next 'real' jewellery should be something dear to you – small pearl earrings or a link bracelet

or a gold-plated pin which you regularly replace and are part of your continuing wardrobe. Intrinsic value means something with favourites.

I don't believe in the old-fashioned 'real or nothing' school. To me, imitation jewellery is essential to the wardrobe. It has a function *with* real jewellery as well as performing in its own behalf. Before buying imitation designs, study the settings of the real thing. Often it's hard to distinguish a good imitation from the original.

In 1955, I received a diamond circlet pin from the Chrysler people as an award. The diamonds are as real as real can be and I wear the pin with a narrow bangle bracelet made of German rhinestones that cost about $50 and looks so real I'm beginning to wonder about it myself. The diamond circlet is beautiful and valuable. The rhinestone bangle is valuable too – as an example of taste over money, which makes it doubly precious to me and a delight to wear.

Unlike jewellery, clothes can be tastefully combined, whatever the cost. If you have some expensive things, don't feel that your whole wardrobe must be expensive. And vice-versa, don't think that one costly garment will make everything else look shabby. Most of today's moderate-priced clothes have expensive 'thinking' behind them – in fact, probably more than goes into *couturier* designs. In high-priced clothes there is more 'room', as the manufacturers say, for giving you your money's worth in trimmings, finishes, and fabric. Less expensive fashions strive to tell the same story, pared down in price.

The ideal wardrobe is well rounded, with many price levels. Such best-dressed women as Mary Martin and Loretta Young have built their wardrobes on both *couturier* fashions and moderate-priced things off the rack. The incomparable Sophie designs and, of course, wears her own custom clothes. But she wouldn't think of wearing an expensive cotton in the country, and I'm happy to say she augments her wardrobe from my collection.

In 1955, I was named the best-dressed woman in the Professional Women category, which gave me particular pleasure because I was the only one cited who does not wear *couturier* clothes. Everything I own is within easy reach – and mostly my own designs, as you may have guessed.

If all your clothes are inexpensive, concentrate on quality

rather than quantity, aiming for the best possible workmanship in your price range. Forget for the moment expensive fabrics such as silk, which you shouldn't expect to find with any degree of quality in low-priced dresses. Inexpensive jersey will make a better cocktail dress than inexpensive silk, which may look sleazy. It's much the same principle as not wearing mink at all if you can't wear good mink.

Classic, uncluttered lines are the best choice in moderate-price groups. For instance patent-leather pumps can be bought for almost any price and should be judged on simplicity of cut and line. The thing to watch out for is the added furbelows of flowers and bows and doo-dads frequently found in lower-priced clothes. *Dare to be simple!*

You can buy a beautiful linen dress for $35 or $235. Your precision of thinking and understand of exactly what you need and want will lead you to tasteful selections. There is good taste at every level.

The best question to ask yourself when buying clothes and later, when putting them on is, 'Will it be appropriate?'

There's no such thing as the right thing at the wrong time. If you're going to a ball, you must wear an appropriate gown. However much it costs, whatever the fabric, the style must be that of a ball gown. I have designed them in mattress ticking and denim, embroidered with Schiffli lace, reasonably priced and suitable for the most ornate surroundings.

I'm proud to say that the National Cotton Council gave me their 1957 award for luxury use of cottons and for contributing to unusual fashion uses of cottons in terms of fabric and silhouettes. It's another one of my pet projects to glamorize utilitarian fabrics for gala occasions.

Inexpensive fabrics appropriately styled are good taste where lavish fabrics inappropriately styled are not. The style of fashion is more important than its intrinsic value.

Since infrequent social events such as balls are a most usual cause of fashion concern especially when the budget is limited – here is another example of the appropriate choice. If you don't usually attend formal affairs and don't want to spend $400 for a long dress you may wear only once, it is tasteful to wear a lavish cocktail-length gown as long as it is richly embroidered or otherwise adorned and catches the extravagant

If a dress is strapless, it's either a cocktail dress that should be worn after five or else it's a sun-dress and should stay in the sun.

mood of its setting. It is preferable to buy a fabulous short dress which is suitable and can be worn again than to have an insipid long dress you won't enjoy wearing to the ball and will never wear again.

Good taste is not strait-laced nor a matter of balancing a cheque-book and wardrobe cleverly. There should be a little madness too – as long as it's *quixotic* and not *psychotic*. Enormous raccoon slippers are an example of what I mean. They're an extravagance but they are also practical, comforting, and warm. True, you can get the same warmth from a pair of old wool socks, but it's not the same thing. When the weather is cold, fur slippers make you glad to be home, glad of an opportunity to cuddle your feet in luxury while also warding off sniffles.

Another thing to consider when dressing for any occasion is how you feel physically. If you've just recovered from a cold and still look a bit peaked, it is inappropriate for you to wear a *décolletage* to a party, even though it's not inappropriate for the occasion, because your skin isn't quite up to par and you haven't the radiant glow of health necessary for bare clothes. At a time like this you would look much better in a complete cover-up such as a high-necked jersey with perhaps satin accessories to fit into the party mood. This way you can be comfortable, covered, and glamorous – and protected against draughts which might send you back to bed for two weeks.

It is also bad taste to wear a dress that is too tight.

I consider suntan as a layer of fabric. In winter show your suntan if you're lucky enough to have one, but if your shoulders are pale and colourless, cover them up in winter and save the *décolletage* for after your next session in the sun.

As for flagrant bad taste, there aren't too many examples. Shorts on a city street is one of the worst. This shows a lack of self-respect and a contempt for the people who are properly dressed. Tourists are the worst offenders. Ill-mannered clothes are as much of an insult to a city's hospitality as they are to private hospitality. Strapless dresses in town are as bad. If a dress is strapless, it's either a cocktail dress that should be worn after five or else it's a sun-dress and should stay in the sun.

Slinky *femme-fatale* dresses are tricky because if they do their job, other wives will resent you. If they somehow 'just miss', you will embarrass yourself and your husband besides.

Eating with gloves on is a phenomenon of manipulation usually attempted by young women trying to 'look elegant' in long white gloves. Wielding eating utensils with gloves is in the same class as playing the piano with gloves – a vaudeville trick.

On the whole, good taste is a reflection of our own culture and our own particular time in history. Fifty years ago, gentlemen were advised to pick their teeth gracefully and ladies did not smoke at all – much less on the street. Always there have been professional influences on the formation and development of taste. Today, in America, the message is passed along by hundreds of fashion editors of newspapers and magazines who inform and advise their thousands of readers, by retailers who pick and choose from each season's collections, by the saleswomen who work with individual customers on selection and fit. Among the individuals who influence taste in America are:

Eugenia Sheppard, who has become a kind of go-between in the American fashion market, interpreting the needs of American women for the designers and manufacturers and interpreting each season's fashion trends and how they should be worn for the women who read her column.

Virginia Pope, the indefatigable world traveller who unearths fashion trends in faraway places and shows how they can best be translated here.

Eleanor Lambert who has fostered American *couture* and encouraged an 'American' flavour instead of slavish adaptation of French trends.

Tobé, whose advisory service to department stores has heightened style interest throughout the country so that the smallest retailer and the largest store can plan according to expected trends.

Taste and money should not be regarded as separate entities, nor will emphasis on one necessarily assure the benefits of the other. Taste well expressed means money well spent. And vice-versa.

SEVEN

The Art of Being
al Home At Home

'What you wear at home should blend in with the décor.
You are the picture, your house the frame'

The biggest challenge I ever had to face as a hostess in my own home was the time Edward R. Murrow visited us via 'Person to Person', bringing some 20 million viewers with him. Under normal conditions, a husband's support is the most reassuring thing a hostess can have. On this particular occasion it was more gratifying than ever to hear a deep, calm voice saying, 'Don't worry, darling. Everything will work out fine'.

When Mr. Murrow's office originally set the date, my first thought was exactly the same as if I were having an especially important dinner party: 'What on earth should I wear?'

If ever I wanted to make an impression, it was that night. I wanted all the people I knew and all those I would face to meet me as a living, breathing woman with a husband and home; not Anne Fogarty as a mere name on a label. I felt a little bit like a bride coming to her husband's home town for the first time.

It was June and I had just finished designing my autumn collection. Having found recognition as a designer with a predominantly full-skirted look, I was changing over to a predominantly slim silhouette for the first time. In discussing what I should wear, my husband said he thought I should appear in a slim dress as a preview of my new beliefs. But after a good deal of soul-searching, we realized a slim dress might hamper my movements and make it awkward for me to sit and stand up gracefully, especially under the unnerving eyes of live cameras. Furthermore, it would contradict my two essential beliefs about at-home wear: *One*, I never wear a slim dress at home; *two*, I never wear a street dress at home.

Now there *are* slim at-home dresses, but they're just not my cup of tea. The long, tight dinner skirt is a beautiful fashion for the right girl in the right home. Sitting and standing gracefully are the paramount construction requirements of at-home wear. I would never sacrifice glamour for comfort, yet the most beautiful ensemble that I would be uncomfortable in would not be much good either.

My final choice was an Old Faithful, a long, full-skirted white wool gown, striped with grey-silver and gold lamé, which has been a perennial favourite. We might be welcomed into millions of other homes, but we were nonetheless in our own home *being* called upon. I knew that I would be relaxed in Old Faithful and that I could forget what I was wearing and concentrate on the blinking red lights and greeting the people beyond them.

It turned out to be exactly right, a time when instinct and reliance on proven values pair off. The slim silhouette would have been torture because I was literally wired for sound! There were batteries and gadgets hidden all over me. A microphone was pinned underneath my bodice and a belt with little motors on it was slung around my hips under my dress – making me feel like a lady cow-hustler with a gun holster. There were other batteries flapping against my thighs and I was told that if my dress had been slim I would have had to tuck these batteries inside my stockings.

Before the programme began, the director had objected to a white dress against the white walls of our apartment, and he very nearly cringed when he saw the woolly texture and muted stripes. But there was no time to change and to our combined relief, the dress looked fine. I must confess I was pleased to be proved right. After all, white-against-white is one of the things that made Homer Winslow famous and it's one of my favourite texture combinations.

Being on 'Person to Person' was one object lesson in poise and dress that I shall never forget. It brought home to me in crystal-clear detail the theories of mobility and ease which I have always believed are essential to hospitality – to being really *at home* at home.

Entertaining is an important part of wife-dressing. As a matter of fact, hospitality should be a continuing influence on your at-home wardrobe whether you're expecting company or not. Dress habits are like table manners. Both must be part of you all the time, not turned on when somebody's looking. Too often women use the excuse, 'We're not going anywhere or expecting anyone', to look dreary and unkempt in the name of relaxation.

I'm all for letting your hair down, as long as it's neatly brushed, and for kicking your shoes off, as long as your feet are well-groomed.

The secret of the natural-born hostess is simple. She is thoroughly relaxed in her own bailiwick. She is *always* dressed for at-home with herself, her family, or unexpected callers as well as for planned entertaining. Hospitality is an innate talent that can be nurtured to serve you well as a woman, wife, and mother.

May I also say that I believe in *long* at-home clothes – pants, dresses, or skirts. They create a mood of comfort, enjoyment, and companionship which reflects on everyone especially your own family. This should not preclude shorter lengths if you prefer them. Ballet styles have become an American classic. Also, full skirts which hit just below the knee have appeared in at-home designs. Whatever length you go to, be sure it does not look or feel like a street dress – or the whole point of at-home clothes is lost.

My personal preference for hostessing is a long, one-piece dress in a cosy fabric such as jersey or flannel in solid colours, patterns, or plaids. For being at-home with the family, though, I prefer long pants with a comfortable top and I am particularly partial to coveralls.

In choosing your at-home 'look', be sure the style is not too voluminous or you'll be knocking ashtrays off low tables as you move. Nor should it be so slim that you can't sit or sprawl. Nor should the fabric be so heavy that you suffocate. Ease of movement cannot be emphasized enough.

Long dresses, because of their traditional role in history and literature, are the visual embodiment of femininity, which is why I've always been partial to them. My private crusade for the future is to restore their popularity on the American home scene.

Another point to keep in mind is that what you wear at home should blend in with the decor. You are the picture, your home the frame. Home may be your husband's castle, but you are the royal homemaker who garbs it and keeps it in running order. The colours, fabrics, and lines of your furnishings reflect your taste and outlook on life as much as your personal wardrobe.

A good approach to co-ordination is: Whatever you're buying, keep a picture of the whole in your mind. If you're slip-covering a couch, think of the range of colours you might be wearing when you sit on the couch. (Nor should you forget your husband and his favourite dressing gown or smoking jacket and how they will look.) Vice-versa, when you're choosing new lounging pyjamas or a hostess gown, conjure up a mental image of how you will look curled up in the big chair near the window or across the tufted bench beside the fireplace.

In recent years many homes have acquired both summer and winter slip covers which are so well made that they don't even look like slip covers. I think of them as home-fashion and as such should be changed fairly often. It's illogical to think that your wardrobe should change all the time but that home furbishings should be expected to go on for ever.

Also, if you've made a mistake, don't live with it. If a chair cover upsets the proportion of a room or causes your husband to mumble under his breath every time he sees it, don't torture yourself or him. Don't live with your tragedy. Re-do the chair.

No woman purposely wastes money. Each of us is very careful when selecting fabrics for furnishings. But sometimes a mistake is made and my position is: Correct the mistake right away! The money spent now to right the wrong will be spent later anyway.

While at-home clothes may vary widely in style, I feel that I must repeat the chief element they all must have: 'femininity'. Many times I wear a long 'camise', which has a low, shirred neckline front and back, short sleeves, and a high waistline with the fabric flowing freely to the floor. In essence, it's the *Recamier* look and can be worn with either flat or high heels. I also wear a drawstring bodice, a long gathered skirt, and a wide, tight belt for a peasant effect. Or, if the Oriental mood strikes me, I accent the eye with liner and wear a kimono.

Lavish brocade and lightweight silk kimonos worn long and straight with matching or gold mesh slippers are fine for hostessing. Cummerbunds, or obis, are beautiful but a problem to me. They look great in photographs but I have found them difficult to manage. They frequently get in disorder and need to be continually adjusted. Unless you're an expert, omit that part of the Oriental costume.

Fancy pants are wonderful fun. As with kimonos and all other at-home wear, you must scrupulously avoid any intimation of sleepwear. Fabrics should be glamorous. Lamé. Brocade. Heavy satin, plain or embossed. Velvet is marvellous in any colour except black because it picks up lint. If you adore black velvet, be sure it's lint-brushed before each wearing and avoid furry-finished tops.

Styling should be extravagant, the over-all ensemble being one you could not possibly wear outside your own home. And remember, as a wife, you have outgrown the dungaree set – except for actual country and beach wear.

You can top pants with any number of things. A silk shirt, a cashmere slipover. A jersey. Since the pants are the featured fashion, the top should be restrained in design or made of matching fabric.

Don't get the pants so tight that you can't bend or sit. I remember my first pair. They were a heavenly blue satin that I had bought in Italy. I had not worn them abroad and, once back in New York, I decided they were just the thing for our first informal party, where we planned to bore our friends with stories of our trip.

What with rushing around and talking to this one and that, I realized that I had not once sat down. After everybody had served themselves from the buffet and I filled my own plate, I chose a low pillow to perch on while I ate my dinner. The next sound to be heard was the shriek of a seam being torn asunder I 'sat out' the party in a pair of Paisley coveralls.

To me, coveralls rank with frozen vegetables as two of the happiest results of World War II. While Winston Churchill's famous siren suit was a contributing influence, I must confess my real inspiration came from the best-looking man I have ever seen in my entire life. He was a filling-station attendant in Naples, New York, a few miles from my mother-in-law's country home, and he looked so marvellous in his mechanic's coveralls I thought they were custom-made.

Possibly it's the way he carried himself, but at any rate, I admired the coveralls and he got me a pair from the supplier in the smallest possible size. I wore them for two summers, with sweaters and scarves, belted and loose, until I adapted them in black corduroy for a story in *Life* magazine.

Since then, coveralls have been part of my fashion story, winter and summer, autumn and spring; in jersey, flannel, brocades, wool, cotton; in solids, Paisleys, and printed designs. It's a garment idea I love and hope to make a classic in every woman's wardrobe.

Straight up and down with narrow legs, a coverall can be worn loose or belted in tight. I generally start off belted and then, like most women, the minute I've eaten, my 18-inch waist expands. In coveralls I can take off my belt after dinner and still look dressed in a casual way.

On to specific kinds of entertaining. Let's begin with that most worrisome of assignments: a dinner party for your husband's boss or important business associates.

I realize it's easy for me to sit back and counsel you to be relaxed. However, there are ways to achieve even that. In fact, once relaxed, you'll find you might even wind up enjoying yourself.

Group your worries into two major categories: your household and your own personal appearance. The two are interdependent. The most glorious dinner will pall if the hostess is bedraggled. Cleopatra herself would have had a rough time beguiling guests, had the food been poorly cooked or badly served.

While labour-saving gadgets have made domestic help theoretically unnecessary, I believe it is worthwhile to have extra help for important parties. Your husband may laughingly refer to you as 'chief cook and bottle washer', but your duties as hostess require you to mingle, not eavesdrop from the kitchen.

The hostess sets the mood of the party. Unless you're enjoying it, nobody else will. If necessary, simplify your menus slightly to take up part of the financial slack. A course omitted, a less expensive wine, will never be noticed in the enjoyment of a dinner faultlessly served and a hostess who is charming and at ease.

An extreme but rather delightful example of this kind of thing happened to us on my one and only visit to London, where we were invited to dinner by a young nobleman and his wife. A uniformed maid announced dinner. Exquisite china graced every place setting in a dining-room of Edwardian splendour. A serving-man with immaculate white gloves brought in the gleaming antique silver serving dishes. His lordship did the serving and dinner consisted of hot dogs, baked beans, and sauerkraut 'in honour of our American guests'. Franks and beans never tasted so good!

Remember, nothing is worth special effort if it *looks* like special effort. But if you feel like serving dinner yourself, then have

Because it's business there's no reason to melt into the wallpaper in order to let your husband shine.

a helper in during the day to do the cleaning – including the silver – and help prepare the basic foods while you work on table arrangements and the flowers. Nothing puts me in a party mood like being and living with flowers.

Flowers should express your personal touch. There's no need to spend lavish amounts. A bunch of daisies, for instance, are wonderful. I think flowers should be fresh and real. There are beautiful artificial flowers to be had and you may combine them with real ones, but only for an arrangement that's not to be seen too closely. Fake flowers are most effective at a distance. On a stairwell. Atop a console in a dim hall.

Roses are my favourite flowers. When I first met my husband, he was the proverbial struggling artist and could only afford to buy me a single rose. Through the years he's continued this practice, and I always have one red rose by my bedside. I loved the idea so much I tried to carry it over to a shelf in the bathroom. It became too expensive having two American Beauty roses every three days – which is the longest they live – so I tried an artificial rose. The light was too strong. It looked harsh and dead. We're back to the one rose in the bedroom.

But to return to the self-service hostess, be sure your menu can be prepared readily and served easily from your place at the table, not from the kitchen. Your place is with your guests. For a more profound interpretation of this, may I recommend Ralph Waldo Emerson's essay, 'Make It Your Own Gift', which says 'The only gift is a portion of thyself'.

As important as the food and service is, what you, the hostess, will wear. By all means be as pretty and vivacious as you can. Because it's business there's no reason to melt into the wallpaper in order to let your husband shine. Present the family just as it is. Furthermore, a sudden change of personality would unnerve your husband, such as being deathly quiet if you're usually full of beans. And you certainly don't want your guests to wonder what your husband ever saw in you!

VIP'S ARE PEOPLE! They're not creatures from Mars. They will respond the same as anyone else to a sincere welcome and a pleasant atmosphere.

As in the case of Ed Murrow's visit, I always wear something tried and true for this kind of entertaining. I want my mind to be free. I don't want to worry for one second about a dress and whether it really does look all right from the back.

Long or short, a hostess dress should have a festive air. I don't like black at home, except for pants or a velvet top with bright, flowing skirt. White or off-white is most elegant, perhaps in a long silk shirt-dress or jersey camise. At home you have a kaleidoscope of colours from which to choose. Make certain your choice holds up under artificial light. A creamy salmon with turquoise jewellery. An electric blue with masses of white pearls. A brilliant plaid with chunky gold.

Since business associates are nonetheless people, think of them as individuals and how you, as their hostess, should look and act to put them at their ease.

Jumping a step further, if you are the boss's wife, entertaining his junior associates, take care not to be too lavish in your personal appearance. A silver lamé gown with an armful of diamonds and emeralds will intimidate the other wives and make for a general uneasiness, however golden is your heart beneath the silver lamé.

'Empathy' is a word used in the advertising business to describe putting yourself in someone else's shoes to see how he will respond. It's a good hostess word too. Try thinking of yourself through your guests' eyes and you will have a much clearer idea of the role you will play.

But no matter what you do, sometimes there is a disastrous evening, a party that never gets going, a series of catastrophes that makes you believe in witches. Once things start going wrong, it's like a runaway steamroller. It's happened to me and the only course I can recommend is to grit your teeth and muddle through.

In retrospect, most disastrous evenings have been the result of slipshod planning rather than gremlins in the woodwork. Leaving details to chance will work most of the time, but when it doesn't – duck.

Not too long ago I lived through one of these nightmares. I enjoy telling about it because it's like having been through a shipwreck: I've survived to tell the tale.

It all happened when our baby was a month old. Somehow or other I found myself giving a dinner party. My maid of seven years quit because our family had become 'too large' – by about six pounds of baby!

Her replacement, inexperienced in my household, began preparations by asking how many wine glasses there were. I

said 12. A trip to the cupboard revealed barely seven. There were going to be eight for dinner. I went out and bought one more wine glass. Suddenly there were going to be ten people. I raced across town and bought two more glasses. Originally a gift, the wine glasses were rather expensive which will explain why I was replacing them in one's and two's instead of buying another dozen for good measure. In the long run that's what I should have done. The very day of the party, the guest list jumped again to make a total of 12.

There's something about trouble that makes me more determined than ever. Maybe I should have painted measle spots on my face and called the whole thing off. I didn't.

It was 5.30 in the afternoon when I got to the glassware store, just as it was closing, to buy the additional glasses. Being in a frantic hurry, I asked the clerk to wrap them in a paper bag instead of packing with the usual sawdust and newspaper. Next having forgotten to order flowers, I dashed into the florist's on my way back home and slammed my package down on the marble topped counter. The glasses were crashed to splinters. The glassware store was by now closed. The florist was nearly out of flowers. At this point, if I could have, I'd have joined the woman's auxiliary of the Foreign Legion – provided they'd take me before dinnertime.

Don't think disaster stopped there. The man I had hired to serve dinner was an hour late. When he did finally arrive, I forgot to tell him about the tricks of our poodle, Peppy. The first course was put on the table too close to the edge, and suddenly we heard a loud crash from the dining-room as those red and green pears my husband adores splattered all over the dining-room floor.

We had dinner at ten o'clock.

While there was no reason or one culprit to blame for the chaos, I naturally blamed the whole thing on the dress I had on that night. I never wore it again. In fact, I gave it away the next day. It may be foolish superstition but I felt that if I wore it again I would relive the agony of that experience. Viewed honestly, I know the evening was a shambles because I was caught off-guard. I had left my planning until too late and then, with eight strikes against me, the glasses broke, the flowers had been sold, the hired help got lost.

Other kinds of hostessing cover a wide range of activities from committee meetings to back-yard barbecues. Here are some

Be gay. Be comfortable. Be mobile. If you're working with splashy food. wear an apron that fits in with your ensemble. Otherwise NO APRON!

general suggestions – plus my personal preferences – for what to wear in various hostess situations:

1. Club or committee meeting

If it's an afternoon meeting at your home, wear a simple daytime dress of the kind you would normally wear to a restaurant for lunch.

If the meeting is at night, wear either a casual daytime dress or conservative at-home clothes such as a long tailored skirt with a classic cashmere sweater.

Your appearance should be friendly, not frivolous.

2. Formal sit-down dinner

Becoming more popular with the rebirth of dining-rooms, it must be done properly or not at all. For a gala dinner to celebrate a friend's wedding, your husband's promotion, or your own tenth or twentieth wedding anniversary, wear the most glamorous long dress you have, short of a ball gown. A formal dinner party can't be a halfway affair. Your invitations should specify black tie, and you may be sure the ladies will welcome a chance really to dress up.

3. Informal indoor buffet

Just about anything goes. Fancy pants. At-home separates. A long dress. An Oriental kimono. Or even lounging pyjamas, which is another fashion idiom that has been allowed to lapse from common usage. I'm all for lounging pyjamas for informal parties as long as they don't look like sleepwear.

Be gay. Be comfortable. Be mobile. If you're working with splashy food, wear an apron that fits in with your ensemble. Otherwise NO APRON! An apron is a fundamental design, created like man and woman, for a purpose! That purpose is to protect and enhance. For hostessing you can't have one without the other.

4. Outdoor barbecue or lawn party

Express your own personality to its fullest. Outdoor entertainment means warm weather, so the range is wide, with only one restraint. Unless you have a swimming pool, don't wear a bathing suit. If it's a warm day, choose something sleeveless or backless that won't crush and look frumpy after an hour or so. You'll feel cool and collected if you look unruffled.

At night, fancy pants, velvet shorts, a long Swiss-dotted skirt, cotton coveralls – it's hard to make the wrong choice in your own back-yard. One caution: If you're doing the cooking, choose something fairly slim and wear an amusing asbestos apron to protect you from sparks.

5. Impromptu supper

If you've been to a fancy Saturday night at the country club or a charity ball in town and you've brought a few people home for scrambled eggs, you may wonder if it's proper to hop into the bedroom and change.

It depends on what you're wearing. If it's a big dress with lots of fabric that will be hazardous or difficult to manage in the kitchen, start your husband pouring the brandies and quickly change. Be sure it's a fast change; otherwise it's rude to leave people sitting around waiting for you.

If your dress is quite manageable, then cover it over with a large, practical worklike apron such as an ordinary chef's apron of the large canvas type. A utility apron is fun in contrast to an elegant gown, for which you quite naturally do not have a suitable regular apron. If you're lucky enough to have anyone help make the supper, be sure to have other aprons handy.

6. Unexpected and last-minute guests

If your husband is in the habit of giving you ten minutes' notice – or no notice at all – don't waste energy being angry. He's actually giving you a compliment because he is completely relaxed and has confidence in his home and your hospitality. So be pleased by this attitude and organize your household and wardrobe for flexibility.

If you have ten minutes' grace, change your clothes *first* and worry about food when the doorbell rings. They'll be happier to wait when they're asked to do so by a charmingly garbed hostess.

If unexpected guests simply drop in and you feel you'd like to change, by all means do so. They can be left to amuse themselves for ten minutes while you dress and collect your thoughts.

I think the male of the
species has deprived
himself of gay plumage
long enough.

The etiquette of unannounced visits varies in different parts of
the country and, believe me, I don't know all of them. So, if it's
customary to 'just be in the neighbourhood', be prepared for it.
On the other hand, unless you enjoy having a 'halfway house',
with people popping in all the time, be sure your friends and
neighbours understand your personal feelings.

If you have other plans, say so.
If you must get to bed early, say so.
If you're not feeling too well, you might have your husband or
family make your apologies.

A SOLEMN MESSAGE TO HUSBANDS:

As lord and master of the hearthside, you should dress your
part as host. Instead of just changing your shirt and wearing
a regular suit, you should begin to build your own at-home
wardrobe. This does not include paint-stained khaki pants or
baggy grey flannels with an open-necked sports short. I firmly
believe that what is needed in masculine elegance is a return
to the rich fabrics, high colours, and luxurious comfort of past
eras which the men of today certainly deserve.

Playing host seems to be a sartorial blind spot with men who
have special clothes for everything else. I think the male of the
species has deprived himself of gay plumage long enough.

A SOLEMN MESSAGE TO WIVES REGARDING
THE SOLEMN MESSAGE TO HUSBANDS:

I can't at this thinking even dare to advise you on how to go
about building this part of the male wardrobe. All I can suggest
is that you as a wife tackle it from your own angle, with one
cautionary word: CONSERVATISM. If you start slowly, you
might wind up being married to Beau Brummel himself, and
all his own idea.

A possible first item is a velvet smoking jacket in a dark colour,
or perhaps a colourful but traditional lounging robe. `

My own husband, surrounded by fashion as he is – aside from
being an artist – is one of the most conservative men I know.
When the pink shirt was *the* fashion expression for men, he
refused to wear one, although he admired it on others.

Very recently a red cotton lounge jacket captured his fancy. He bought it and has adopted it for at-home wear.

His enjoyment is evident every time he wears it and I hope this will lead him to other things.

❦ ❦ ❦

EIGHT

The Wifely Art of Courage and Discretion

'If all-white endows you with an ethereal quality, don't begrudge the time and effort essential to its care.'

It is my belief that all wives are *not* alike. The men in the grey flannel suits might address us as if we were all turned out of the same mould, but as far as I have been able to see among the thousands of women I have met and known, the only things all wives have in common are husbands – and a wish, I hope, to make them happy and proud of us as women.

The art of courage and discretion is a clarion cry for individuality, a turning away from slavish adherence to every fashion or beauty trend. Courage and discretion go hand in hand: the courage to dare to be yourself, the discretion not to overdo; the courage to do something unusual, the discretion to temper it.

When it comes to clothes, most of us think subjectively. I confess that when I look at a dress, I automatically think first, 'How will I look in it?' But being a designer, I then judge it in terms of other figures, other proportions, other complexion and hair tones.

As a wife, you have only yourself to consider when it comes to fashion. Study your figure and colouring. Know what suits you and what doesn't. However divine it might look on the cover of a fashion magazine, don't buy it if it isn't really you.

My fashion philosophy, one which is expressed in my collections as well as my personal wardrobe, is the understated 'Natural Look'. While I like to be noticed, I don't want the gasping double-take. I am against the Witch Doctor and Kabuki Dancer schools of outlandish make-up and costumes. Hallowe'en comes once a year and that's quite enough for me.

Courage and discretion have much to do with your powers of *omission* rather than *commission.* It takes an intimate sense of balance to pare down an ensemble so that the essentials show through, instead of obscuring it with a lot of distracting extras. As examples, charm bracelets should be worn on one wrist, not both; if there are fancy buttons, let them be the focal point without other adornment; don't obscure a beautiful neckline with a distracting necklace or beads.

You are what you are and fashion can only mould you. Your hair, your face, and your sense of styling offer endless opportunity for expression. Colour, in particular, offers an enormous palette.

When I was a child, one of my mother's friends visited her often, and I always thought of her as being on a pink cloud. This may partly be explained by my active imagination and a tendency to dramatize, but as I think back, she *was* on a pink cloud. She never appeared without some bit of pink near her face, reflecting a rosy tone in her complexion.

She had many pink hats, some with short veils that danced across her nose. She wore pink blouses or pink beads or a scarf or a flower in her favourite colour. I called her 'The Lady in Pink', and perhaps in my childhood fantasy pictured her in pink chiffon sipping pink champagne.

If you have a pet colour, a certain shade of blue, a radiant salmon tone, use it, wear it, insinuate it into your wardrobe. Reach the point where your husband and friends automatically give you presents in that particular colour; think of it in terms of you as a kind of personal trade-mark.

Trade-marks are a good example of courage and discretion because they express individuality yet avoid being 'outlandish'. Perhaps the most successful personal trademark in recent years has been the black beauty mark on the face of the famous fashion model, Jean Paget. The beauty mark is real, and at first she tried to cover it with make-up when posing for pictures. A photographer convinced her not to and this tiny bit of dark pigmentation has set her apart in the modelling world, which is jammed with beautiful faces.

Trade-marks are many and varied. The Duchess of Windsor never changes her hair style. The fashion editor of a national magazine wears a fresh rose every day. Princess Grace of Monaco won't be caught dead without her little white gloves; Mary Martin has become synonymous with the close-cropped cut; Greta Garbo started slouch hats 20 years ago and they still carry her stamp; Mamie Eisenhower brought back bangs in 1952 and they're still with us.

Every trade-mark mentioned has attracted notice by repetition. Doing something once doesn't make it memorable. As you

A two-foot cigarette holder or a leopard on a leash is a bit hard to take even once, much less as a permanent accessory.

can see from the Garbo hat, the Grimaldi gloves, and the rest, a simple accessory can, in time, become your special 'thing' among your friends and family.

But, may I repeat, avoid the outlandish. A two-foot cigarette holder or a leopard on a leash is a bit hard to take even once, much less as a permanent accessory. Recognition is the chief asset of a trade-mark, but make it something natural to you, something that is easy to make part of you. If you have to work at a trade-mark, it loses its naturalness and becomes an affectation.

Virginia Pope has a trade-mark that I call an 'Aura of Hat'. She always wears a hat and they are made of many things – flowers, ribbons, feathers, veilings – but somehow they always seem to blend into her hair so that hat and head are one.

Another fashion editor, Bettina Ballard, always wears a snood-type hat, which covers all her hair. She must have hundreds of variations in different colours and fabrics to blend with her wardrobe. I have the feeling that this is so much a part of her that she must even have special ones for lolling in the bathtub.

A trade-mark can be jewellery too, and can last for a season or a lifetime. A friend of mine knew her husband when they roller-skated together as children. For an anniversary gift he gave her a gold skate key which has become a distinctive, if sentimental, part of her attire. An Englishwoman who married an American and came here to live had difficulty getting used to the central heating. It was always too warm for her. She began to buy sleeveless dresses to beat the indoor heat. Gradually her wardrobe became almost exclusively sleeveless, a style line she enjoys and sticks with. Not that she's a fashion stick-in-the-mud. It's just that when the new silhouettes appear, she looks for the sleeveless versions.

A trade-mark, as you can see, is a means of expressing courage and discretion – but only if you are so inclined.

Perhaps the most widely used trade-mark is the 'Natural Look', which has become second nature to most American women and sets them apart when they travel. In essence, the 'Natural Look' is functional and decorative. It is both the easiest and the most difficult look to assimilate, which is where the wifely art of courage and discretion comes into full play.

You must have the courage to try new fashions and the discretion to reject those that are unsuitable or adapt them to suit your image. I have a friend who wears nothing but shirt-dresses, in every fabric, weight, and colour. Even when the chemise came in, she stuck to her guns and found a shirt-dress version of it.

You must have the courage to accept into your wardrobe items that need special care and the discretion to find out beforehand the kind of care required. This way you won't wind up with a winter-white that won't wash or clean or a pale leather bag that has to be dyed black when it gets dirty.

Courage and discretion will help you beat the elements when they act up just as you're leaving the house. Be adaptable enough to dress as originally planned, with a layer of protection over it, or to change into something else that expresses the same idea and can better cope with the weather.

A turning point in my career came from just such an incident. I had come down with bronchial pneumonia just before Christmas of 1955 and spent most of the pre-holiday season in bed while everyone else was partying. There was one special party, a yearly ritual that I didn't want to miss. After much cajolery the doctor said I could go if I dressed properly. It was a freezing night and I didn't dare risk anything low-cut. Instead I wore a pink-and-white-checked wool shirt-dress with the neckline plunged to the waist and filled in with a pink chiffon. I wore fur-lined boots and carried pink satin sandals in the shopping bag that contained the Christmas gifts bought for the occasion.

Among the guests at the party was Adam Gimbel, the president of Saks Fifth Avenue, who told me later how much he liked my ensemble. That night's necessity to be both warm and festive has deeply influenced my subsequent thinking. When I joined forces with Saks two years later, I thought back to that Christmas party as the beginning.

Shakespeare's Polonius might have had courage and discretion in mind when he said, 'This above all, to thine own self be true'.

If the night is cold and you want to be glamorous, don't shiver in something *décolleté*. The goose pimples won't keep you warm. Wear *something warm*.

If all-white endows you with an ethereal quality, don't begrudge the time and effort essential to its care.

In other words – have the courage of your convictions as a woman and the discretion of your experience as a wife.

THE WIFELY ART OF COURAGE AND DISCRETION 85

NINE

Am Wife —
Will Travel

A WORD TO HUSBANDS:

'It is better to live rich than die rich.'

SAMUEL JOHNSON

Whether you're touring the national parks, attending a convention with your husband, or hemisphere-hopping via the North Pole, there are two hard essentials that can lighten your travels. Cold ruthlessness and steely nerves – the unseen but much-felt basic requisites for planning a travel wardrobe.

Well, maybe not *too* cold and steely, but do be very much in control of your destiny as well as your destination. The wear and tear of travel will be a continuing challenge to your judgment, ingenuity, and stamina.

Before any trip, study your travel itinerary as if you were a logistics expert. Consult your travel bureau. Ask people who've been there. Make notes on climate, time of year, type of places where you'll be staying. Then – and this may sound like a contradiction but isn't – THEN analyse all this information and translate it into your own idiom. The friend, for instance, who tells you to take lots of bare cocktail dresses for the evening knows what she's talking about for herself; whereas you may be just as dressy in all-covered-up pastel wools.

More than in any other area of fashion, travel demands clear-cut decisions before you leave and adaptability once you're on your way. Not only can't you go home again for a forgotten necessity, but it may be impossible to replace or improvise during your journey.

Since you can't take your whole wardrobe with you – unless you live in a caravan – the decision must be made well ahead of time as to exactly how you want to look on your trip, what fashion demands will be made on you, what fashion demands you will make on yourself, and how restrictions of time and facilities will affect not only your looks but your comfort.

After your arrival is not the time to discover that your suitcases might just as well have been lost for all the good they will do you.

To be a logistics expert, do like the man from Gilbert and

Approach travel from
the viewpoint of comfort,
co-ordination, and
emotional value.

Sullivan – make a little list! First, write down all the clothes you would *like* to take, including accessories. Completed, it would probably fill a steamer trunk; so, with the maximum outlined, start crossing things off until you reach the almost-bare minimum, constantly asking yourself which dress can do double – or even triple duty with accessory changes. Which coat can express day or evening? Which bags can say the most and take up the least room?

Once at rock-bottom minimum, you can then add the few goodies that will really make your travel wardrobe. For me they include a frilly negligee, an extra evening gown, additional swimsuits, or extra sweaters.

For you, they might be anything. Don't leave behind with regret something important to you, even if it doesn't belong in the accepted travel wardrobes we read and hear so much about.

This leads me to the raft of so-called 'Basic Travel Wardrobes' available from department stores, airlines, travel bureaus, and so on. I don't know who writes these macabre little guides, but they are either men who wear the same suit for ten years or women who have never travelled. The sad part about them is that a lot of usually knowledgeable people throw their fashion know-how to the winds and obey the clinical advice given. Rather than presume to suggest how many dresses or sunsuits or slip-overs you personally should take on your next journey, I will approach travel from the viewpoint of comfort, co-ordination, and emotional value.

Every traveller is different. Every trip is different. It would be as foolish for me to outline a wardrobe in detail as it would be for you to follow it step by step. Europe in summer is different from southern California; winter in Vermont or Switzerland or Phoenix, Arizona, contrast spiritually as well as climatically. My travel wardrobe for a recent visit to Paris on vacation was entirely different from that of the designers' for Leonard and Andrew Arkin, my associate firm, who go to Paris two or three times a year on business.

A travel wardrobe is personal. It will change from trip to trip. It is a condensation of your regular wardrobe, not a separate entity. After all, you're still the same person whether you're at home or far away, and you'll want familiar garments with you. *Never cut your gear so close to the bone that you leave your personality behind.*

The first thing you have to get along with is the climate. It won't go out of its way for you. Be prepared for the worst as well as the best. Florida, for instance, can seesaw between 50 and 80 degrees on alternate winter days. Autumn in New York is notorious for spurts of torrid Indian Summer. In much of the Southwest the temperature drops about 20 degrees in 20 seconds when the sun sets behind the nearest mountain. Wherever you go – big city, large mountain, sandy beach, or bright little island   anticipate being a little colder or warmer than you expect.

In winter, remember that it is winter, except on a tropic island in the Caribbean. Don't take a complete summer wardrobe. The days will undoubtedly be warm enough for sun wear, but from cocktail time on, the air is cool, the time of year winter. Wools and jerseys are not merely apropos – you might freeze to death in organdie.

Formal wear in the tropics is quite formal. If you're planning to cover the elegant spots, take a chic ball gown. Some of the most beautiful evening wear in the world turns up in the Caribbean.

Most official travel wardrobes ask you to get along with two or three pairs of shoes. I personally would rather stay at home than travel with three pairs of shoes. Last year, for a ten-day rest at Boca Raton, I brought 18 dresses and 20 pairs of shoes. 'Dresses' includes everything with a skirt from the little cabana dress I wore on the bus to the beach club to a lavish evening gown for dancing at night. 'Shoes' included beachwear, pastel pumps, and evening satins. I do not believe that the ratio of shoes to dresses was the least bit uneven.

Imaginative switching of dresses will serve you well while travelling. On the trip just mentioned, I wore one of my favourite jerseys on Saturday night with satin shoes and again the next day to church with neat kid accessories.

A friend of mine went on a cruise to Venezuela with her husband, and included in her wardrobe was a simple backless salmon-coloured linen which she planned to wear for one of the less formal evenings on board. To her chagrin a passenger at her table turned up for breakfast in a duplicate of the dress in a different colour worn with flats, a kerchief, and a straw bag. Her first thought was not to wear the dress at night, but then she decided to follow her original plan. That same evening she

wore it with gold sandals, gold jewellery, and a pale satin coat –
a good example of interpretation.

If you are flying to your vacation, overweight luggage may be
intimidating you into taking a wardrobe like a prison matron's.
It's amazing to me how many people will spend thousands – or
at least hundreds – on a vacation yet limit their baggage to
the prescribed 44 or 66 pounds. The point is that these weight
restrictions are for *free* transportation. If you're willing to pay
for the extra poundage, you can take as much as you like. The
added cost should be regarded as a legitimate travel expense,
not something to be avoided at all costs. Magical places lose
their magic if you know you're not dressed as well as you might
be because of the weight limit.

Lingerie is another thing that the travel bulletins advise
limiting to two or three 'complete sets', as they usually
phrase it. This is another area where I think you need *more*
underthings and nightwear than necessary. If it's a vacation,
you're not supposed to slave over the washbasin. If you're on a
business trip you may not have time. Personal laundry service
is rarely good or fast. Save yourself grief. Have more than
enough lingerie.

Travel irons cause more arguments than politics. Some people
swear by them; some grow pale at the mention of their name.
I'm betwixt and between. When I bring one I'm glad that I
did; when I don't I find that I can always borrow one or find
someone to iron for me.

A few summers ago some friends rented a big house on the
Long Island shore for the summer and invited us out for a
week-end. It was a pretty casual household and most of the
equipment was hidden or non-existent. On Sunday morning I
awoke early and decided to iron the four petticoats I intended
to wear for church (petticoats were the big fashion note that
summer). I crept into the kitchen, couldn't find an iron or an
ironing board, and returned to our room where I had a travel
iron. Smoothing down my side of the bed, I began to iron.
After a few minutes Tom woke up, startled. Not only did he
think he was in church but in heaven because all he could
see was this mound of petticoats and all he could feel was a
delicious warmth.

WHAT TO WEAR UP IN THE AIR

For short hops, wear something loose-lined, such as a straight up-and-down shirt-dress that is belted in tight on *terra firma* but released for comfort aloft. Even if you feel fine, your stomach expands with altitude. You'll need room in your apparel in order not to feel constrained.

Jerseys and tie-silks are ideal travel fabrics, as are the many miracle and combination fabrics. Many miracle fibres marry well with natural fibres for amazingly strong, resilient, and beautiful fabrics. I will discuss miracle fibres more fully later in this chapter.

I'm not mad about suits for travel because they're too confining, with the exception of a well-tailored tweed for the depths of winter. More and more fabrics are travelable because of processing. In the depths of summer linen, which used to be taboo because it was always one big wrinkle, now comes through unscathed because of 'tebilizing'.

For 'jumping the pond', as the pilots call the oceans, or sitting up for a long cross-country haul, carry something in your tote-bag or folded inside an extra coat to wear during the flight. Once the Fasten-The-Seat-Belt sign has been turned out and the plane has levelled off, go to the ladies' room and take off the dress you want to have fresh on arrival. Give it to the stewardess, who will hang it up. Change into something comfortable and cosy – it's usually cold up in the air – such as a wool smock or some loose coveralls that will allow you plenty of leg and body movement. Most airlines give you little woolly slippers for long hops, so take off your shoes too. Or tuck your own lounge slippers into your tote-bag.

For sitting up all night where you're travelling in darkness, it's perfectly all right to change into a long tailored robe of the kind you might wear before unexpected callers at home – just as long as it is designed to stay closed while you curl up for sleeping. A coverall could be a great idea too, giving you plenty of leeway to find a comfortable snoozing position.

On our first trip to Europe in the summer of 1953, petticoats were at their peak and I was determined to wear them, bulky or not, starting with the transatlantic flight. My going-away ensemble was a brown linen with a tight waist over four petticoats.

I remember some of my fellow passengers were making bets on my getting in and out of the ladies' room, but I proved how flexible they can be. Later, getting into my berth, I simply stepped out of all four petticoats at once and stood them cone-shaped at the foot of my bed.

What proved to be an adventure were the 18 more petticoats I had packed in a separate suitcase. Among other things, we were going to a ball in Ireland and I needed three long crinolines for my ball gown alone.

After some experimentation I had found it was possible to pack all 18 petticoats together like jack-in-the-box coils.

We arrived in Ireland at six in the morning and the first thing the customs inspector wanted to know was, 'What's in that bag?' I explained it was my 'Crinoline Case'. Perhaps it was the early hour, but this reply upset him. 'Like this . . .' I explained, backing away and showing him the edges of the crinolines I was wearing. He looked at me as if I were mad and insisted that the case be opened.

I knew just what would happen. It did. All 18 petticoats popped out as if released from school. The inspector helped us repack them.

Everywhere we went, I left my calling card as it were – in Ireland, where I traded some for a few Connemara shawls; in France, where the late Jacques Fath demanded one in return for a glorious shawl of his design.

When I returned to New York, I had lots of shawls but not one single petticoat. Distributing them wherever we went was kind of a fashion Marshall Plan.

Sea travel falls into two categories. Either you're in transit, which means you need clothes for both the ship and wherever it is you're going, or else you're on a cruise, which means everything will be sea-oriented.

For in-transit travel a practical technique is to have separate baggage for each part of the trip. Suitcases for the voyage only can then be checked at the distant shore, to be picked up for the return trip, while on-shore bags can stay in the hold of the ship until needed.

Automobile travel permits the smallest and most easy-to-care-for wardrobe, especially if you use car cases that hang straight in the back seat. Wear a full skirt, which does not bind the way

Whatever the season, carry a heavy topcoat. Weather is almost as tricky as political situations.

slacks might, and will also be acceptable wherever you stop to eat or sleep. At the end of a long stretch on the road, you'll feel less fatigued if you look presentable when you get out of the car. It's human nature.

The year after our first trip to Europe we took to the road to see America. My car wear consisted almost entirely of seersucker shirt-dresses in various colours and fabric patterns cut straight up and down for maximum comfort. With them I had leather belts and matching shoes to slip on the minute we stopped. Whatever the current fashion silhouettes, the full skirt and straight-up-and-down shirt-dress are classics that go on and on. Wife-driving or wife-sitting-beside-driver requires style mobility in crush-resistant fabric.

The wardrobe you take for a motoring trip depends on the kind of trip you've planned and whether or not you're taking the children. The elements are at you every moment in a car, so protect your head, skin, and eyes with attractive covering.

With jet travel getting us places practically before we've left home – and letting us pay later at that – world travel has become more than an idle dream. For the average two- or three-week holiday, you can go practically anywhere. Whichever direction you head, here are a few geographical fashion hints to help you plan your travel wardrobe:

EUROPE

Whatever the season, carry a heavy topcoat. Weather is almost as tricky as political situations. July in Paris might be blistering hot in a pavement café at noon and have bitterly freezing rain by night.

In Italy, Spain, and Portugal, your dress must have sleeves for church. I discovered this personally one Sunday in a village outside Madrid where a peasant woman saw my sleeveless though high-necked dress. She tore her shawl in half in order to cover my arms. To my surprise many women worshipped with their heads uncovered. Customs vary, it seems. In the United States it's the head that must be covered; in Europe it's the arms.

(P.S. You can be arrested for wearing a two-piece bathing suit on a Spanish beach.)

England is well known for its lack of central heating. If you find it beyond valour to creep into icy sheets, ask for a hot-water bottle. Bed socks and a warm nightie might be advisable for touring Britain, even in summer. If you look at the map you'll see how far north the British Isles are and the weather can be cold and damp.

Formal requirements vary in the different European cities. In Paris a black tie is demanded in certain elegant restaurants, such as Maxim's on Friday night. In London the famed Café de Paris will shunt you to the balcony if you're not in evening dress. Dress regulations change frequently, so inquire at your hotel for the latest word on what you're expected to wear.

Another very important time to make local inquiries on what to wear is when you are invited to a private home. Customs differ abroad and it is inconsiderate to ignore them. I made the mistake myself by arriving for 'informal lunch in the country' wearing what I considered beautiful slacks and shirt, only to find everyone in quite formal luncheon clothes – a forgotten tradition in America. My sister, who has gone around the world several times, made what she call 'a prize boo-boo' in the new republic of Ghana. She and her husband were invited to luncheon at a government official's home. Because the weather was so warm she wore a simple cotton. To her embarrassment she found herself an honoured guest and everyone wearing the latest exotic creations from Paris.

Garden parties and afternoon teas outside the United States generally mean 'Wear a dress'.

As for clothes etiquette in general, Americans have a reputation for scantiness which is rightly resented. Pope John XXIII, when he was Cardinal Roncalli and living in Venice, once commented wittily about the scantily clad visitors who swarm the city in summer: 'People need not come to Italy in furs or woollens. They can come dressed in that modern American silk, fresh and soft, which is a veritable refrigerator at low cost. Italy, on the other hand, is not on the Equator, and even there, by the way, lions wear their coats, and crocodiles are lined with their most precious hides'.

BERMUDA AND THE BAHAMAS

Being English, there is an air of casual conservatism by day, formality by night. Classic shirts, Bermuda shorts, and pleated skirts for sports and touring the islands; pale silk and linen

sheaths for lunch or tea; full-length or cocktail dresses with
your best jewellery at night.

CARIBBEAN ISLANDS

Very casual and colourful play clothes by day; flamboyance at
night according to your mood.

MEXICO

In most parts the days are warm, the nights are cool. The cities
are cosmopolitan and you wear dark, sophisticated city clothes
according to season. Shorts and slacks are taboo in the cities,
though naturally play clothes are suitable for resorts. Formal
dress is seldom needed. Since part of Mexico is in the tropical
zone, a raincoat is a necessity.

UNITED STATES

I can't possibly attempt to cover the whole country – that
would be a separate book – so here are a few generalizations.

New York, Chicago, and Los Angeles are very hot in summer.
Most hotels and restaurants are air-conditioned, so have
necessary cover-ups. San Francisco is cool all year round.

White shoes are out of place in most big cities unless they
match a white dress. Hats are worn for luncheon both winter
and summer in smart restaurants.

If you're going to a city for the first time, find out its dress
habits beforehand. Dallas is one of the best-dressed cities in
the country; New Orleans goes in for formal fashions; San
Francisco is extremely chic and has been called the Paris of
the West. Washington has a flavour of international glamour;
New York and Palm Beach each attract international society;
Los Angeles has the flamboyance of the film colony. Chicago
supports many fashionable shops; Boston and Philadelphia
tend towards the traditional, Atlanta, the fluffily feminine.

The list could go on and on.

RESORT WEAR

When discussing resorts, I always think of Groucho Marx's
quip: 'I met my wife at a travel bureau. I wanted to get married
and she was the last resort'.

The subject is so wide, I could write an entire book on resorts alone, analyzing each separately. There are summer resorts and winter resorts; places to take the children or go with a group of friends or hide away alone for a second honeymoon.

The best way to prove your skill at wife-dressing can be summed up in three little words – 'Know your resort'. Don't blithely plod ahead, *assuming* that one place is the same as another: FIND OUT from people who've been there, from the travel department of your favourite newspaper, or write to the resort itself.

Each has its own identity. At one you may change six times a day. At another you may look like a beachcomber or a ski bum all day and emerge a princess at night. Speaking generally, however, I return to the old refrain: 'Bring too many changes rather than too few'. As noted earlier and worth emphasizing again, extra shoes add more than their weight to a travel wardrobe. (Shoes are my personal whims. They give me the feeling that my selection of clothes is limitless.)

Furs are to my mind a little ostentatious for most resorts unless you need a hearty fur coat for warmth. For warm-weather resorts, limit fur expression to trimmed sweaters or as a collar on a pastel coat.

CONVENTION TRAVEL

As a convention wife accompanying her husband, or as a delegate in your own right to a business of organizational pow-wow, your travel wardrobe has to be absolutely right. Once you arrive, there won't be time to buy anything. Since conventions take place all over the country – in mountain resorts, at the seaside, and in all the big cities – there's no such thing as a standard convention wardrobe. Let the agenda be your guide. It is printed well ahead of time, so study it *before you* leave home, not while travelling. Will you tour a factory? Listen to a speech at a beach lunch? Attend an elaborate tea? Dance in a rose-strewn ballroom?

As you study the programme, make a list. As on any other trip, once you've noted everything you could possibly wear, start paring down, but not to the bone. A convention is both hard work and hard fun. Have plenty of changes, again stressing more-than-adequate shoes. The feet are the first part of the body to tire and they can drag the rest of you down with them.

If you'll be sitting at meetings or seminars, choose comfortable daytime dresses that not only look well but sit well. Bring plenty of stockings; they have a way of catching on things at conventions. Maybe it's the change of air. Likewise plenty of underwear. Unlike vacation travel, conventions leave little time for personal chores even if you enjoy doing them.

SHOPPING

It's always fun to buy new clothes away from home. Somehow the shops in faraway places seem to be bursting with goodies that you have never seen back home. I have a split personality about it: in theory I don't approve, yet I do it all the time and enjoy myself thoroughly.

Often the question arises whether to travel with half-empty suitcases and buy what you need to wear on the scene. This I think is dangerous because you might arrive on August Bank Holiday in England or De Gaulle's birthday in France or a special saint's day in Ireland, Spain, or Mexico and find the shops closed.

By all means, supplement your wardrobe with unique additions acquired on your travels. Choose carefully so they are not onetime white elephants. Have a special thought for lighting. The brilliant blue that looks so wonderful on the sparkling bright Mediterranean shore may be too harsh for the softer light of Minneapolis or Detroit.

Abroad, the most enjoyable shopping is in the local equivalent of the dime store and in the flea market. There you can pick and choose, enjoy the thrill of discovering a regional delight, and haggle over the price into the bargain.

PACKING

Years of needlessly crushing my clothes through careless, hurried packing have finally taught me a few things about the delicate art of fitting a two-foot pile into a case one foot high. The technique is a little like the clowns in the circus who squeeze themselves into a midget car.

Some general packing suggestions

Carry a tote-bag containing toiletries, cosmetics, and accessories that you may want at a moment's notice. Toilet articles should be housed in spill-proof containers.

Pack the heaviest things at the bottom of suitcases close together to prevent sliding.

Spread large garments smoothly with as few folds as possible. Pack snugly with no loose corners.

Put shoes in individual plastic or cloth bags among your other things, or carry all shoes together in one case or small duffle bag. It is worth the trouble to wrap each shoe separately in tissue.

Attach clearly marked tags to all baggage, including your tote.

THE QUESTION OF MATCHED LUGGAGE

One of the first material signs of getting on in the world is matched luggage, a favoured gift to graduates, brides, and oneself. With travel so fast and so frequent, matched bags have become less important because luggage takes such an awful beating.

Rather than being a matter of taste, matched luggage is important only if personally important to you. I have a friend with magnificent all-white leather bags. She polishes and cares for them as she does her shoes because she enjoys the luxury of good leather and is willing to spend time on it.

In my own case, I had admired some plaid suitcases for quite some time. My husband bought them for me for my birthday and I used them almost at once. They were so badly damaged by unavoidable rough handling that I've become disenchanted.

My pet baggage story happened on a fashion tour. I was waiting at the airport with my model, Penny, for our bags to come through. When the porter asked her which were hers, she said, 'Over there . . . the set of matched luggage – those four brown boxes'.

While I wouldn't go so far as to travel in brown boxes, I do think it's a good way to carry a big evening gown with lots of skirt. Packed separately in a sturdy dress box from a department store, it will remain uncrushed and be lightweight.

There is a kind of inverse snobbery to mangy-looking baggage that can sometimes go too far. Don't look like a gypsy with tattered leather and broken straps in the hope of looking like an experienced traveller. As for stickers, their snob appeal has long since gone because packages of travel stickers can be bought. Also, you might get into trouble if you let baggage tickets accumulate. When you get off the plane in Chicago, your bags might be waiting in Detroit because of a left-over tag from a previous junket.

THINGS TO LEAVE AT HOME

1. Big Hats unless you're going to Ascot or another definitely big-hat event. You'll be spending too much time 'mothering' an unwieldy hat box.

2. Umbrellas unless it's the small, foldable style. Forego your long-handled umbrella unless you're addicted to a walking stick.

3. Breakable bottles rely on tube packages of toiletries and cosmetics as much as possible. Carry the rest in non-breakable containers. Perfume bottles may be Scotch-Tape-closed and carried in individual airtight containers. Be especially careful of perfume in the air; pressure plays mean tricks. If perfume spills on your clothes, you've had it.

4. Active-sports equipment this, of course, excludes the amateur champ en route to a tournament. Unless you're on a sports holiday, rent your equipment as you go along.

5. Bulky bathrobe sheer wool takes up one-tenth the room and gives all the needed warmth.

6. Household supplies some people still think you need to take toilet paper, soap, and heaven-knows-what to Europe. You'll find everything you need or a reasonable facsimile in most hotels or procurable for you by a willing bellboy.

7. Heavy books if possible, find what you want in pocket editions, which weigh little and can be thrown away.

8. Worries on vacation, you want an open mind to absorb what you see; on a business trip you'll surely find new ones.

THINGS TO TAKE

1. Your diet Be indulgent but don't go hog-wild and eat yourself out of shape. You'll be miserable when you get back.

2. Credentials better than your bankroll are letters of credit and other credentials to enable you to cash cheques. Without these you can be uncomfortably stranded.

3. Your favourite perfume however much trouble, you must have it.

4. Bath accessories nail brush, washcloth, or sponge, the daily bath items you won't find in a hotel. Keep them in a waterproof bag.

5. *Sewing kit* one with scissors and different-sized needles plus threads for a split seam, a slipped hem, or a small hole in a stocking.

6. *Band-Aid* I never seem to use them at home but once I leave, I'm a mass of nicks and cuts.

7. *Collapsible plastic hangers* ideal for drip-dries without snagging or leaving rust stains; necessary outside of the United States, where many hotels do not furnish enough hangers.

8. *Scotch Tape* wrapped around your hand, it brushes away lint as well as, if not better than, a brush.

9. *Pet accessories* this doesn't mean empty out the drawer. But do take extra gloves, scarves, and your favourite jewellery such as beads or earrings. It's impossible to decide exactly on accessories before leaving, so give yourself some leeway.

10. *Bed socks* altitude, change of climate, fatigue, lack of central heating all make your feet cold.

To sum up, make travel broadening not burdening. You can live out of a suitcase if you've packed with care and imagination.

TEN

A Faint Cry in the Wilderness or Pardon Me While I Breathe Fire

*'I adore artificial flowers on hats —
the more the merrier, especially
daisies and violets.'*

This being my first book, I can't resist the opportunity to sound off on my personal pet peeves. A faint cry in the wilderness of conflicting opinion, they are strictly my own viewpoint and, as they say on television, do not necessarily reflect the ideas of anyone but me.

Some of these foibles have to do with fashion; others concern the home, parties, and just plain living in the same world with other people.

Getting things off your chest is supposed to be good for you. The mere contemplation is enough for me. I'm feeling better already. So, pardon me while I breathe fire on:

THIN PLASTIC RAINCOATS THAT COME IN BAGS

They make me feel inhuman, like a head of lettuce inside a vegetable bag waiting to be stashed away in the refrigerator. There's no reason to look like a badly wrapped cellophane package in the rain. It's not as if we walked for miles and miles in wet weather. Mostly, we have to dash a few steps from the driveway to the house or up the street to the bus stop or other transportation. Modern coat fabrics are made to withstand moisture if you're caught in a sudden drizzle. Otherwise, dress properly for the rain in any of the many coats and capes that are either frankly raincoats or specially treated to be water-resistant.

While I'm on the subject, those plastic covers for men's hats also unnerve me. Men's hats are a covering in the first place. Why have a cover-cover?

WEARING CURL PINS TO WORK OR TO GO SHOPPING

How can there be pride in being a woman if your head is covered with tiny bumps that are only accented by a bandanna bandage?

While not wanting to sound like a soap-box orator, I do think it borders on dishonesty to use an employer's time for personal grooming. If you need a half-hour away from your duties to unpin pins and comb out the curls, you haven't arrived ready for work.

As for shopping, it is impossible to judge a new dress from the neck down when from the neck up the reflection in the mirror is something from outer space.

Not being able to do a thing with your hair is a universal problem, but there are other ways to solve it besides being a human pin cushion. Have your hair cut so that if the curl dissolves, it will look reasonably well straight. Have an alternate hair style, such as a French knot or a chignon, that can be used when all else fails.

Try 'quick-set' short cuts such as one used by one of my models. She has short, straightish hair. When its gone limp and she has only an hour to do something about it, she rolls it up in tin curlers, dampened first under the tap. The damp curlers in the dry hair creates a miraculous curl in a very short time.

Perhaps most detrimental is the effect on husbands. Wife-dressing, after all, includes wife *hair-dressing*. The eventually lovely hairdo will not blot out the image of the hair-set. I'm not about to say that marriage is a Technicolor film where husband and wife are perfectly groomed at all times. Naturally, before a big party or some other special event, you may want to pin up your hair for a last-minute set. But this should be the exception, not the rule. If you must put your hair up and be seen that way, invest in a frilly or flowery mob cap for glamour and your husband's sake.

DIRTY WHITE GLOVES

White gloves are only effective when they're snowy, glisteningly WHITE. If you like white cotton gloves as much as I do, wash them after each wearing. Stifle the impulse to put away a pair that you've worn because 'they don't look too dirty'. They will, as soon as you put them on again.

COLOURED WIGS

I may have my own head handed to me, but they remind me of Madame Tussaud's Wax Works. My credo is naturalness, and pink foam curls or pale blue waves do not 'naturally' belong on

Handkerchiefs have always been a leading feminine weapon, a widely accepted cliché for attracting attention by fluttering or dropping to the floor.

a human head. I think fancy-dress coiffures belong at fancy-dress balls.

TISSUES INSTEAD OF HANKIES

Now, don't get me wrong – I wouldn't know what to do without paper tissues. I carry them with me always, have them in my workroom and in the kitchen and bathroom at home. Incidentally, I match colours to decor there.

What bothers me is to see a beautifully groomed woman reach into her elegant evening bag and fish out a paper tissue. Handkerchiefs were designed for use in public and a pretty one, sprayed with perfume, is a small but truly feminine accessory. With it you create an aura of loveliness. Handkerchiefs have always been a leading feminine weapon, a widely accepted cliché for attracting attention by fluttering or dropping to the floor. Don't leave them at home. Have at least two with you always and USE THEM.

Tissues are ideal for repairing make-up in the powder room or for any other personal use including a quick buff to shoes, if needed.

Tissues and hankies each have a separate function. Tissues for utility; hankies for coquetry.

LIPSTICK STAINS ON TABLEWARE

This may reinstate me with the tissue people because I think it is the height of bad manners to begin a meal with a heavy coating of lipstick on your mouth. Glasses, cutlery, linen napkins are glaringly smeared with red, which is not only unpleasant to clean but looks terrible while the meal is in progress. If you wear heavy lipstick, blot it before mealtime with a paper tissue.

UNDERWEAR STRAPS THAT SHOW

Unless you're Gypsy Rose Lee and want to prove you're wearing several layers of clothes, avoid this grooming flaw by sewing strap snaps in the shoulders of dresses that give you this kind of trouble. A slipped strap can be the one false note in an otherwise perfect fashion composition.

PERFUME THAT ASPHYXIATES

Aroma is supposed to drift in on those around you like a

morning haze, not be a knock on the head. Scent is subtlety, not a sledge-hammer. Women who say their perfume leaves a man panting are quite right: they're choking him to death. The minute he can find some fresh air, he'll escape.

A delicate manner of using perfume is to put some on a dab of cotton for the inside of your bodice, a small amount sprayed along your shoulder line and up each side of your neck, and a quick squeeze for your hair. Sachets of the same scent kept among your underwear, scarves, and hankies will permeate them with a faint hint of aroma that is 'you'. Winter furs take kindly to a once-over-lightly spraying once or twice during the season – although over-spraying may be hard on the life of the fur.

OVER-ARRANGED COIFFURES

Like a symphonic arrangement of 'Mary Had a Little Lamb', they are admirable because they're difficult, but are better not done at all in most instances. The exceptions here are the rules, such as the woman who has her hair coiffed every day at the hairdresser because she is on display much of the time and must be sumptuously groomed.

FATTENING FOODS AT A DINNER PARTY

Contemporary life is geared to keeping slim for health and vanity's sake. A hostess should take into consideration her guests' possible preference for foods that are low in calories. Now, I'm not for a minute suggesting that all dinner parties should degenerate to watercress on Melba toast. What does concern me is rising from a dinner table straining against my clothes and feeling uncomfortable for the rest of the evening.

LONG, TAPERED DRAGON LADY FINGERNAILS

I believe shorter, shapely, and well-manicured fingernails fit in with modern fashion. Nail polish should blend with your lipstick.

While on the subject of nails, I might as well mention feet. To coin a phrase, women flip off their shoes at the drop of a hat – and I'm well aware of being one of the worst offenders. What makes this a dubious trend is unmanicured toes. Even through stockings, unkempt toenails present a pretty unpleasant sight.

IMITATION FLOWERS ON CLOTHES

I can't explain why exactly, but it rankles. Facsimiles of a rose or violets or daisies give me a feeling of depression rather than a pick-me-up, as if I couldn't afford the real thing. Imitation of realism saddens me. On the other hand, highly stylized flowers in self-fabric or lace or organdy, which have no pretence of being the real thing, add tremendously to attire. The old cliché of a little nosegay of forlorn forget-me-nots on an Easter suit sends me into a scurry.

Yet I adore artificial flowers on hats – the more the merrier, especially daisies and violets.

TOO MUCH MAKE-UP IN THE DAYTIME

It makes your whole image harsh and detracts from whatever lovely clothes you are wearing. Sunlight accentuates every crease, every artifice, especially on the beach where you must be most careful of make-up. From cocktail time on, exaggerated make-up is great, especially false eyelashes, which are frankly fake and therefore fun. They are not supposed to be real, *are* not an attempt to delude anyone that the lashes have suddenly grown two inches overnight. In artificial light dramatic make-up can be worn most effectively; by day, take it easy. Sunshine and daylight are very cruel to a brittle *mask*.

HANDS YOU HATE TO TOUCH

Poets of old wrote about milady's hands. Today they might have trouble finding even a pair of them. I have talked about nails; now, my annoyance is aimed at hands that could so easily be smoothed with a quick dab of cream, that could be protected from nicks and stains with household gloves. Fashion begins with a well-groomed body. Remember, hands are part of the body.

STOCKINGLESS LEGS IN THE CITY

If the legs are whale-belly white, the over-all look is disastrous. If the legs are tanned, there are still areas of whiteness or mottled colour around ankles and heels and on the backs of the calves.

If your legs are too tanned for stockings, use a small amount of make-up to blend the colour and give a matt finish. To prevent the flaky look that a *heavy* tan gets, rub a thin layer of oil on

A woman wearing sun glasses indoors or at night looks like nothing more than a satire of a Hollywood glamour queen — grade B.

your legs and then dull that with the barest coating of make-up – about as much as you would use for a face foundation.

EXTREMES OF AIR-CONDITIONING OR HEAT

Like someone searching for a smiling fortune teller, I am looking for a happy medium, too. It's a sad reflection on the machine age that in summer you can get frostbite from air-conditioning and be steamed alive in winter.

CHARM BRACELETS AT THE THEATRE

I love charm bracelets – but if anything heats my blood to boiling, it's watching a movie or listening to a play punctuated with the jingle-jangle of somebody's arm moving up and down. Whereas the old silent movies showed signs that said 'Ladies Will Please Remove Their Hats', I'm all for a notice in today's theatre to read 'Ladies Will Kindly Remove Their Charm Bracelets'.

DUNGAREES AS REGULAR WIFELY GARB

Except for camping out at a beach cottage, dungarees have no place in wife-dressing. Pants must be perfectly styled to flatter the female figure. Dungarees, by definition and price, cannot be exquisitely tailored. Leave them to the youngsters.

SUN GLASSES INDOORS

Unless under a doctor's orders to be a lady in the dark, a woman wearing sun glasses indoors or at night looks like nothing more than a satire of a Hollywood glamour queen grade B.

ELEVEN

Some Very Personal Answers to Some Very Personal Questions

'Wife-driving is important to wife-dressing . . . you can choose your car coat and other regulars in your wife-driving wardrobe to blend with your chariot'

A WORD TO HUSBANDS: *Never ask a question unless you are prepared to take the time to listen to the answer.*

When it comes to fashion, every woman has a personal question or two. They can range from how to cope with certain emergency situations to specific problems in dress and family relations.

In the past ten years I've met thousands of women at forums, luncheons, charity teas, and while making personal appearances at department stores. The first personal question I'm usually asked is how big my waistline is. After that, questions are many and varied. Here are some of the most-asked questions with my own personal answers.

What should I wear for house-cleaning?

First of all, something you would not be ashamed to be seen in by your husband or an unexpected visitor. Nor should you dismiss your personal impact on the children. You'd be amazed at how deeply they respond to your appearance. A child psychologist asked a little girl what she thought of her mother. 'A dust mop', she said. It developed that her mother's daytime costume was always a kerchief hiding her hair, a house dress, and a dust mop in hand or in sight. How you look at home affects not only your own spirit but the spirit of the entire household.

Secondly, something that gives you complete freedom of movement. But at the same time you mustn't forsake a girdle and bra, which give necessary support to your active body.

I could recommend all kinds of household wear. To begin with, it should be protective and attractive. A one-piece coverall in a washable fabric is great, but don't think I'm a pants addict entirely. I like skirts that have plenty of knee action without being too full. Voluminous skirts get in the way and may cause accidents.

Protection means covering your body from accidents and cleaning ingredients, especially the legs. You may enjoy trotting around the house in shorts, but you tempt fate with your vulnerability. Your body includes your face, so a foundation film and lipstick are important to keep your skin moist and your lips smooth and to catch dust particles that fly through the air. Also, use work gloves for heavy tasks.

Wear comfortable shoes; which doesn't mean heavy ones. I work at home in ballet slippers. If I wore Oxfords, my feet would be falling off in ten minutes. Whatever the footwear, be sure it's bright and neat. Don't wear old scuffed slippers or down-at-the-heel daytime shoes. They're bad for your feet, and demoralizing too.

Bandannas are wonderful if worn with style. Have a wardrobe of household kerchiefs to go with what you're wearing. Try a bright calico wrap-and-tie dress with a fetching kerchief to look as sprightly as Brigitte Bardot in a recent film where she wore a tri-cornered kerchief tied under her chin with a wedding gown.

For really heavy household chores, wear dungarees with a neat cotton shirt and maybe a red bandanna. I don't like dungarees for casual wear, but since they're the best thing for messy jobs, wear them with authority.

Don't look like a steam-fitter or a garage mechanic when what you are is, purely and simply, a wife.

When my husband asks me what I want as a present, should I tell him to surprise me – or should I ask for something inexpensive, hoping he'll spend more?

What woman has not said, facetiously and with a grain of hope, 'Well, I'll have a mink coat!'

That out-of-the-way gift-giving between husbands and wives is a very intimate thing. I adore surprises and have found that the old-fashioned hint dropped here and there will take root and flower. My husband has wonderful taste, and either magically remembers the things I've admired or asks one of my close friends for advice.

Surprises may be hazardous, but usually a man spends more on them than on specific things you may want.

Anniversary gifts are very special, and I think it's more fun to discuss the presents you will give each other. Like trips, planning is as enjoyable as getting something new. For a fifth anniversary for instance, you might discuss the possibilities of something in wood, which could be anything from a cottage by

The rib cage is perhaps the most neglected part of the female anatomy.

the sea to a bamboo necklace. Some people say it's the thought that counts. I think it's the planning together.

Making notes about things you would like is a good idea if you can manage it. I always think of things in the bathtub or when I'm half-asleep in the middle of the night. I rationalize my not getting up with the notion that if it was such a great idea I'd remember it without writing it down.

I can never look like a fashion model, but how can I know when I have the best possible figure?

Most husbands would rather you didn't look like a fashion model because they're too emaciated-looking. The truth is that most fashion models are not emaciated. They simply have a small, narrow bone structure which is impossible to achieve by dieting. Since photographs have a tendency to make the figure look larger, the narrower the figure, the better.

You as a wife don't have to worry about the camera. Proportion – or an illusion of proportional balance – is what makes a well-formed figure. Learn by trial and error which lines and in what direction do most to create the illusion of perfect proportion. Some points to study are:

If you have a short neck, wear your collars open, favouring the V-line for elongation. If you have a long neck, don't wear a deeply slit bodice.

Whether your arms are overheavy or overslim, be sure sleeves fit snugly. Loose sleeves accentuate the arms.

If you're very thin, don't think a loose belt is going to make you look fuller. You'll only look like a potato sack.

Full skirts are ideal for both very thin and very heavy figures, provided there is a well-defined waistline. If there is no indentation between ribs and hips, avoid the full skirt. Having been called 'Queen of the Full Skirts', I should probably be the last to say they're hard to wear. What I will say is this: Don't think you can hide under a full skirt. It can add grace and femininity to your walk, but it can also overpower you if it isn't nipped in tight at the waist.

The rib cage is perhaps the most neglected part of the female anatomy. You can't do much about it except understand how its shape can determine the fit of what you wear. Most women understand about the hips, waist, and bustline but the rib cage can create havoc. If it's too small and you have a large bosom, there's the problem of fitting both. If, as is more general, it's too large, you must cope with minimizing its appearance. Waistlines that rise up higher in front than the back of a garment will help create the illusion.

Aside from the changing of fashion decrees, skirt lengths should depend on how long your body is from hip to knee and knee to ankle, also whether your calf starts high or low. Whether current styles are 'longish' or 'shortish', you'll always have an inch or two leeway for choosing the correct length for your leg. Find the most flattering length before a mirror. Then, don't vary the length according to heel height, because regardless of the shoes you wear, the hem still hits the same place on your legs.

If you have made glaring style mistakes in the past that do ghastly things to your figure and accentuate its faults, analyse the clothes and find out why. A certain hip line? A collar style? A set of gathers? Determine to avoid these personal pitfalls in the future.

At what age should I interest my children in fashion?

I believe they're never too young to learn about colour, gaiety, and personal pride in looking nice. The hair ribbon on the tiniest tuft of an infant girl's hair could be a beginning. The textures and colours of baby blankets are the first elements of clothing security an infant gets, and might very well be carried on through other stages.

I'm not a child psychologist, but as a mother I do know that when children reach the toddling stage they are more interested in pulling their clothes off than choosing them. But there is where you may be able to encourage them to stay clothed by coupling a pink and white sweater with a little pink dress or a blue-and-white-striped shirt with blue corduroy rompers.

At this writing, I have only one child – a year-and-a-half-old boy who has a very decided fashion sense, as long as everything is bright red!

Friends of mine who have children a bit older do a wonderful thing which, as I have seen it, I can highly recommend as a way to instil social and fashion responsibility in offspring. Whenever they have a dinner-party, their boy, who is eight and his sister, five, are given their dinner early as usual, and are then bathed and changed into their party clothes.

When the guests arrive at 6.30 or 7pm, the children help to greet them, feeling very festive and part of things because they're dressed for the occasion. Then, when dinner is ready to be served, the children say good night and are off to their rooms. They may have been dressed up for a total of a half-hour, but the experience improves their social awareness and encourages appreciation of clothes and the fun of being dressed specially for special occasions.

By the time they're at school, girls will probably come to you for fashion advice and discussion without being asked. Boys will doubtless consider clothes 'sissy' and only submit under protest to hair-cutting, darning, and replacement of battered play clothes. Fashion re-enters a boy's life when he becomes interested in girls.

Since fads play a big role in the fashion habits of children and teen-agers, your contribution to their appearance will be to see that whatever they wear is in a becoming colour and fits (if the fad permits).

I wear glasses. Do you have any special advice for me?

Well, I wear glasses too, at least for reading, and I think of them as being part of my personality rather than my fashion wardrobe. I do not believe glasses should match what you're wearing because it only draws attention to them. The shape and colour of the frame should blend into your facial tones and hair colouring. Warm, natural tortoise shell and heavy gold frames are flattering to most people. For novelty, I like large bamboo frames for sportswear or leopard-print frames whose colours blend with my brown eyes and dark brows. Normally, I wear black frames in a simple design which seems best on my face and head, whatever I'm wearing.

To me, jewel-bedecked frames are as much of a fashion evil as over bejewelled sweaters – only worse because glasses are worn more frequently. Coloured rims should be chosen with great care. White is wonderful on sun glasses if you are tanned, but should be avoided otherwise because white frames tend to drain the colour from your face. Red frames create the opposite hazard of distracting from your face because of the bright colour.

I think there have been altogether too many bugaboos about glasses, too much 'I wear glasses so I can't do this or wear that'. To my mind, anything you can wear *without* your glasses, you can wear with them. That goes for hair styles and hats in particular, which seem to create the most concern. If veils are comfortable, wear them. They can look marvellous with glasses. If you want to wear bangs or wide-brimmed hats or flowers in your hair, don't sacrifice one iota of your fashion personality because of a pair of frames.

I have red hair and have been told I shouldn't wear pink or orange. Is that so?

No! Red hair is the most exciting colour you can have!

While I'm generally dogmatic about natural colouring, red seems to be the most easily adapted because most brown hair has a good deal of auburn in it. Henna is the least harsh of all hair colouring and is in most cases an intensification of existing tones.

As a redhead, you can wear any colour in the spectrum. Forget the theories about pink and orange. They are your most dramatic colours. Just be careful of tonal qualities. Avoid purplish tones of red or fuchsia because most red hair has amber colouring rather than bluish colouring. Choose your colours in bright daylight so you can be sure of your choice. Pinks with a slight yellowish cast are good. Orange, having no blue at all in it, is always reliable. Pale pink and rust are very exciting.

At night you can try out startling effects such as a bright pink, which with your red hair will create an exotic Gauguin look.

How do you get over that feeling of 'I haven't a thing to wear' when you have a cupboardful of clothes?

This, I'm sure, is a problem which confronts the richest women in the world as well as the poorest, and I'm part of the 'Mrs In-Between' group.

In actual fact, the problem has nothing to do with the kind or quantity of clothes. The feeling of being stranded comes from one of three things – or a combination of them. Your emotions or energies may be at a monetary low ebb. Your wardrobe may lack co-ordination so that there are few complete ensembles. Or you may have everything you need, but the organization of your cupboards and drawers is so chaotic that you can't *find* anything

From my own experience, a low ebb of energy is the most frequent reason for my own sudden feeling of frustration and despair when I open my cupboard door. What I do is forget about what I'm going to wear for a few minutes and lie down with my feet elevated. Five minutes 'on the flat' is the best restorative I know of, along with a cube of sugar, a square of chocolate, or a sweet carbonated drink for a quick pick-me-up to start the vital juices flowing and make decisions that much easier.

Totally depressing and frustrating is a lack of coordination, where you haven't the right shoes to go with the dress or the coat is wrong for the hat you want to wear. Of course co-ordination should begin with the planning stages of your wardrobe and be a continuing influence rather than last-minute patchwork.

As for organization, the time you give to systematizing cupboard and drawer space will be more than made up by the knowledge that when you look them over, you'll find you *do* have something to wear.

Should the family car go with my wardrobe?

In fantasy I see myself with a different car for every ensemble, although I must admit my daydreams never get around to how I'm going to park them all!

Back to the cold light of reality, I think it's more important for the car to blend in with the natural habitat. It should look well in the drive silhouetted against the colour of your house and fit into the colours and shapes of your geographical location as a whole and your own particular neighbourhood or street. Since you are indirectly influenced by your surroundings when you choose your wardrobe, you'll find that, without really trying too hard, what you wear will fit in with what you drive.

When it comes to extreme or off-beat car colours, my only concern about them is they may either bore you or irritate you before it's time for a new model.

Wife-driving is important to wife-dressing, especially with the growth of the two-car family. If you are lucky enough to have a smaller 'second car' for your own use, I won't take back what I said about the colours harmonizing with the horizon; but I will allow as how you can choose your car coat and other regulars in your wife-driving wardrobe to blend with your chariot.

At what age can a woman be audacious in what she wears?

With so much emphasis on youth, here's where I'm happy to say that a little maturity comes into the picture.

It's difficult to pinpoint an exact age, but to be daring in fashion you need the poise and sophistication that comes with experience.

You must be old enough to understand the fundamentals of dressing, to understand the contours of your body in terms of colour and line, to understand the image your temperament and your way of life have created. Like acting, writing, painting, fashion is a skill. You must learn the fundamentals before you can experiment with interpretation.

What do you wear when you're upset?

Instead of fighting gloom tooth and nail, I wallow in it briefly and then set about dispelling the black cloud of depression.

Weather is often the culprit. If it's a dismal, bleak day, I find solace in wearing something white and soothing. Friends of mine swear by colour, and if your spirits brighten when you put on something red, that is your best therapy.

While red is one of my favourite colours, when I feel tired I shy away from it because it's too much of a shocker. So don't take the brighten-the-corner-where-you-are as gospel. It may grate on your already jagged nerves instead of setting them aright.

If you're going out, a tight belt and firm foundation will make you feel alert. Changing your clothes will often snap you to attention too. Don't let your figure slump. It's sure to reflect in your emotional outlook.

If you're staying home, change into something comfortable but glamorous. A sloppy old robe will only make you feel droopier.

Find comfort in pet accessories or frivolities such as a soft fur bag or a favourite scarf or false eyelashes.

BUT if you're really tired and couldn't care less about going out and socializing, the best cure is: Dare to stay home!

For after-five wear, which comes first – comfort or fit?

This is one question I feel very strongly about. I believe that clothes should be perfectly fitted at all times, and the feeling of after-five wear especially should be one of *constraint* rather than comfort. You shouldn't feel as if you're wearing a nightgown when you're in a cocktail dress.

A well-groomed sleeve must fit snugly. A beautiful bodice must have definition. A well-made fashion, correctly fitted, improves your posture, changes your walk, elevates your head, causes you to reflect in your manner the flavour of the dress and the occasion.

For cocktail parties I often wear a dress I would never dream of choosing for the theatre, which means sitting down for several hours – whereas a cocktail party means standing up for several hours. For cocktails I like a dress that I can 'lean' in, a silhouette that looks well standing or mingling with groups of people.

A friend of mine has a pet cocktail dress that she says she can't possibly wear to a dinner party because wearing it she has to either stand up or lie down!

Elegance and queenly bearing go hand in hand with constraint. You're not meant to suffer; but you are supposed to be 'aware'. After-five wear is not meant for acrobatics. You needn't have complete freedom of movement nor room to raise your arms higher than is necessary to comb your hair and dance. Unless you're partying on a yacht, you will rarely be asked to climb a rope ladder.

How do you manage to keep a slim figure?

Being a very active person with narrow bone structure, I have found it fairly easy to keep my weight *down*. But keeping it *trim is* something else again. I believe in wearing a girdle with everything – including lightweight panty styles with shorts and slacks.

Most of my adult life, I've been lucky enough to have an 18-inch waistline, which I'm convinced is because of the cinch or wide, tight belts I've always worn. The theory is very much akin to the old Japanese tradition of binding feet to keep them small. When the loose, beltless look came in, I got lazy and stopped wearing a cinch. In no time my measurement jumped to 19 and a half. Writing this, I'm trying to work it back to normal.

An integral part of fashion is foundation wear. No figure in the world is smooth enough to take a very tight sheath or firm enough to take a clinging fabric. To maintain your figure at its flattering best, depend on foundation garments to control and distribute, a cinch or tight belt to restrain.

Do you think certain colours are better at night than during the day?

Artificial light will bring out slightly different qualities in colour than natural daylight, but rarely enough to make a point of drawing a line between 'day' and 'night' colours. I will qualify this by saying my personal belief is that neutral colours such as light beiges and greys tend to be less interesting at night, whereas dominant colours as well as black and white are fine after dark.

Skin tones are what should determine the colours you wear. As discussed in another chapter, you can alter your skin tone with foundation base to blend with any fashion colour.

Everyone has definite ideas about black and I'm no exception. Since heavy-textured black picks up lint, I prefer to wear it at night. Black velvet is intensified and richened by artificial light. On the other hand, I hate to wear black for cocktails, not because of the light – but because every other woman seems to be wearing black too. If you're addicted to black for cocktails, state your fashion individuality with unusual styling or some sensational accessories.

Although light-coloured clothes obviously need more care, I have a passion for pale blue. It's the most wonderful colour – by sunlight, moonlight or 75 watts.

I have big feet. Can I wear red shoes?

If you like red shoes, wear them! The colour shoes you wear depends on your personality, flair, and the costume you have in mind. Don't be self-conscious about shoe size – and that goes for small feet too. The styling of a shoe will determine whether or not it is flattering.

One exception is white shoes, which tend to exaggerate foot size, but not enough to prohibit their wear with an all-white costume, which could be off-balance with any other colour footwear.

Should shoes always match some other part of your outfit?

Not necessarily. In fact, unless they're coloured shoes that match a dress or suit, it's more chic if they don't match gloves or a bag. For instance if you're wearing a black dress with red shoes, you might wear white shorties and a small gold bag.

❧ ❧ ❧

TWELVE

Never Underestimate the Power of a Man

A WORD TO HUSBANDS:

A word to the wives is sufficient.

It's time to speak up for the men!

Since the first cave man dragged a mate into his lair by her uncoiffed head, the dominance of the male has been recognized as fact. Only recently have there been serious rumblings to the effect that the role of the male – particularly the American male – has been usurped by women.

A growing sport in recent years has been 'malebaiting', undermining the social and emotional status of the American husband. I'm sure I speak for all women when I say I'm bored to tears reading that our men are the most exploited of masculine creatures since the female seahorse discovered a way for her mate to carry the children.

It is said that women pick the houses men inhabit, the cars they drive, the furnishings they live with, the vacations they take, the appliances they use. Since women outlive men, cynics claim that the women end up picking the men's bones and getting all their money.

I say it just isn't so! I am a wife, a mother, and a businesswoman. Because I don't sit home on a *chaise* all day munching chocolate creams but go out to work every morning does not mean that I've taken over the reins of my marriage. It's still very much a man's world and I, for one, couldn't be more happy about it.

If those clever surveys are true if women are so completely self-sufficient that husbands' functions have been reduced to fathering children and perhaps partnering bridge games – then why is it that American women spend millions of dollars every year beautifying and grooming themselves for the express purpose of pleasing MEN?

What's so obviously lacking in these surveys is the intelligence to interpret them. In each of the buying situations mentioned, agreed that women do the *advance* scouting for a house, a car, furniture. Women as the domestic partners in a marriage do much of the actual purchase of food, make most of the arrangements for vacations, entertainment, and finding out when the feature film goes on at the local movie. But for whose approval and confirmation is the wife doing all these things?

Her husband, of course!

She will plod through 50 houses or apartments and narrow the choice to three or four before taking up her man's time and patience. She will collect tons of folders about faraway places before a family confab on vacations. She will buy the food he eats and much of the clothes he wears, true, but only items of his choice.

Further, she will swelter under the hair dryer and stand like a human pin cushion for alterations in order to attain the image that will light up her husband's eyes.

Therefore, never underestimate the power of a man – in society and in the home. Never ask for whom the belles toil – we toil at our toilette for the approval and admiration of our husbands and the general appreciation of men with whom we work or meet in other outside situations.

What does disturb me is that most men cringe at discussing women's fashions. They may say they don't know a bodice from a flounce, but they do 'know what they like'. When they're displeased, they set up a howl that echoes through Seventh Avenue like the voice of doom. A notable example was the 1957 'Sack Look'. Paris started it. American men finished it. Dresses in every price range hailed the shapeless form. But the greeting at home was far from enthusiastic – if not downright hostile.

The 'Sack Look' died aborning, and the American Male taught the fashion world a valuable lesson – while all the time disclaiming knowledge or influence on women's clothes.

Men's simultaneous influence on and disinterest in fashion is a fascinating paradox. Fashion contributes to the well-being of your family. On a larger scale, it is important to the nation's economy. While your husband may take for granted having himself and his family nicely clothed, he may never have considered the extensive range of the fashion industry, which begins with basic fibres, machinery for weaving, cutting, and sewing, and all the intermediary steps, sales distribution, national promotion spreading out across the country in a giant network that reaches into the smallest retail store in the smallest town. Fashion is a basic commodity, not a whimsy.

Wife-dressing is basic to marriage, not a frippery.

Clothes contribute to the livelihood of a community – from the store that sells them, to the service that cleans them, to the places they are worn.

Clothes contribute to the morale of the family too. It would be presumptuous to say that they 'make' a happy marriage but neat, attractive people who are aware of themselves as individuals are usually better able to cope with problems than people who don't much care how they look.

It will be some time before men take naturally to reading fashion magazines as women have taken to men's magazines. In the meantime, a cheering note is the increase of manmade purchases of women's clothing as gifts. Instead of saying, 'Go and buy yourself something for your birthday', husbands are stifling their qualms about entering the inner sanctum of women's fashion stores. Many of the big stores deserve the credit for this trend. At Christmas-time, especially, 'For Men Only' departments have helped overcome masculine hesitation.

While most husbands have always been anxious that their women look right, they've usually relegated the details and sat in judgment on the final result. More and more today, men buy their wives clothes by themselves or go along on shopping trips to help them pick and choose.

When I was in San Francisco for a personal appearance at Saks, a very well-known doctor came into the department with his wife. He wanted to meet me, he said, because he was interested in the personality of the designer behind the fashions. He and his wife travelled a good deal and since he enjoyed shopping with her, she rarely bought clothes by herself.

Personally, I find it thrilling to have my husband pick out something for me to wear. It's a wonderful compliment and proves he is thinking of me and trying to find something that will express my personality. I think a personally chosen accessory or dress or some item of casual wear is much more exciting than a bushel of orchids.

Elsewhere I've mentioned the fur bag my husband bought me several years ago. It is one of my dearest possessions, partly for sentimental reasons, partly because it fits so perfectly into my way of dressing that I use it constantly and am continually grateful to Tom for giving it to me.

If I had bought the bag myself, I'd have felt guilty about spending so much, but Tom's having bought it has given him a stake in how I look, a pride in making a contribution to my appearance – which is after all a reflection of our marriage.

You can encourage your husband's active interest in your wardrobe by suggesting at an opportune time that he might enjoy shopping for something for you. Such as gloves or slippers or some pretty underwear. Men enjoy buying feminine fripperies for their wives, though I'm not sure whether the reason is psychological or sociological.

You may be amazed by some of his first selections, but be brave. In his mind's eye he may be endowing you with qualities you don't possess or a personality trait that doesn't exist. Don't be completely rocked if he comes up with a fringed negligee when you're accustomed to whitepiped classics. He may be thinking that under the quiet serenity stirs the heart of a harem queen.

Wear it if you possibly can, and if it's completely impossible, make a joke of it.

Obviously if your husband buys you something slinky he might welcome the siren influence in your boudoir wardrobe.

It was very interesting to me to learn that the first gift to a woman in most men's lives is a pair of stockings. This, too, may have psychological implications, but I like to think of it as a way of expressing interest in the way a woman looks and giving more lasting enjoyment than a box of candy, which costs about the same.

In the higher financial strata, furs are a man's favourite way of saying, 'I love you', usually in the form of a stole or a cape where fitting is unnecessary, so the element of surprise is assured.

Choosing dresses demands a little more experience and confidence. Most men have architectural vision. A dress creates or completes a preconceived image. My own husband will look at me in a new dress and murmur something about liking the 'dorsal line' – which I now know means the way the back fits.

Discuss your wardrobe needs with your husband, the types of clothes necessary for the social and business obligations important to you both. Many wives go to the same two or three shops for their clothes and, in smaller communities especially, deal with the same sales personnel. Your husband may enjoy shopping for you if he can rely on a sales girl who knows your figure and the general type of styling you prefer.

A good indoctrination might be to ask your husband along the next time you go shopping. It will be like his first trip to the supermarket – a revelation giving him a better appreciation of selection and prices.

Introduce him to your favourite sales girls, who will help him when he comes in on a solo errand. A friend of mine who lives in exurbia and has a houseful of children to manage began a few years ago to ask her husband to select one or two things for her because she couldn't leave the children. Now, he buys practically everything she wears. He and the sales people know each other well. He understands his wife's figure problems, yet he can view them objectively when he considers colours and textures. She adores wearing the clothes he's selected. He is glowingly proud of her appearance mainly because he's playing Pygmalion to her Galatea.

Off-the-record, too, men tend to spend more money when shopping for you, and consider it well spent as a reflection of their good judgment.

To husbands who might like to shop for their wives, here are some things to bear in mind:

Flip through the current fashion magazines for ideas.

Consider the atmosphere in which your selection will be worn.

Find out from your wife – or by looking at the labels in her favourite clothes – where she usually shops and in what department.

In choosing a negligee or other boudoir wear, consider your home setting before making your wife the Queen of Sheba. Or suddenly you'll find her swathed in a long, flowing negligee with huge maribou cuffs in a bedroom barely large enough for the bed. Think twice and if necessary, fulfil your whim to see your wife in maribou by buying a pair of fluffy scuffs.

Fantasy and whimsy are best expressed in the boudoir. If you don't like to see your wife's curlers – and most of us need curlers at one time or other – give her a lush, lacy cap available in the toiletries department of most large stores. She'll feel pampered by being glamorous in her grooming preparations.

Most wives would be more thrilled to have you bring home a pair of shocking-pink lounge pants than spend the same amount on an armful of American Beauty roses.

At-home wear is another area for husband-expression. Most wives would be more thrilled to have you bring home a pair of shocking-pink lounge pants than spend the same amount on an armful of American Beauty roses.

Although if other wives are anything like me, they're greedy and want both!

If you feel confident enough to buy a dress, be reasonably certain that your wife has the accessories to go with it. A colour you've never seen her wear may be hazardous because of the additional expense to accessorize. On the other hand, if you find a new colour you think instinctively is right for her, she'll find a way to wear it. Women are very adaptable.

Aside from general apparel, here is a checklist of fashion items that will endear you to fashion-conscious wives:

Of course a mink coat is heaven, but fortunately or unfortunately most of us are earth-bound. Fur is the most luxurious, most flattering, most exciting, most romantic item of fashion. A shaggy fox muff, a fluffy raccoon bag, a sleek mink scarf, a smooth beaver beret, a striking leopard belt – or some cosy lamb scuffs – *all* say, 'I love you', and cannot help but add a unique touch to your wife's wardrobe.

ACCESSORIES

Every woman has a passion for certain accessories. It may be gloves or handkerchiefs, scarves or earrings. Take your cue from the overcrowded section of her wardrobe. Although she may already have jillions of gloves, one more pair carefully chosen by you is an exciting gift to her.

AT-HOME WEAR

Here you're completely free to pick and choose, expressing your own personality as well as your wife's. Buy her what you want her to wear. She'll be thrilled by your interest.

Since this chapter is addressed to both husbands and wives, I would like to make a few final points:

TO WIVES

By encouraging your husband's interest in fashion, you will be better dressed. Having his advice and participation all along, you will never have to contend with his disapproval at the very last minute which is when most men choose to say, 'Are you going to wear *that?*' If he is partially responsible for the selection and meaning of your wardrobe, he'll take a more realistic attitude towards the money spent and quantity of clothes necessary for the various facets of your life.

TO HUSBANDS

Men who take an interest in fashion seem to have better taste than most women, who are too close to the subject, having grown up with it. You are in a position to give your wife a fresh approach that is both objective and personal. Your taste can add to her understanding of herself. Your approval can add to her self-confidence.

A husband's interest in his wife's wardrobe will add to his understanding of her needs and desires as a woman; a wife's regard for her husband's preferences and judgment on how she looks add up to a happy marriage.

❦ ❦ ❦

THIRTEEN

The Delicate Matter of Bargains

'Write 500 times, "I will think before I buy"'

━━

A WORD TO
HUSBANDS:
'If you keep a thing seven years you're sure to have a use for it'

SIR WALTER SCOTT

━━

To my mind, the 'bargain' has become the most maligned of the joys of life. A true bargain is like a rare jewel – or the first edition of an old book – or the dollar bill you've forgotten in an old handbag.

A bargain cannot be mass-produced, cannot happen every day, cannot be planned in advance. I think that in recent years the real meaning of bargain-buying has been obscured by massive 'sales' and monster 'mark-downs' which promise the moon and usually give only the value for which you've paid. It may be old-fashioned of me, but I believe that you get what you pay for, that heaven protects the bargain hunter only to the dollars-and-cents value of the merchandise.

Now don't think I shut my eyes completely to the possibility of finding a bargain. I don't. I merely put it in the same category as winning the Irish Sweepstakes. You can't will it to happen; you can't count on a bargain when you need it. If the magic wand of coincidence taps you and there before you is just what you've wanted and at an unheard-of low price – grab it, of course!

To me a bargain does not necessarily mean 'cheap'. It does not mean 'reduced in price'. It *is* something you want and need. A ball gown reduced from $200 to $300 is no bargain if you don't go to fancy balls. A dress that costs $50 and looks like $200 is a bargain, whereas a $200 dress marked down to $50 can be a bad risk.

Why? The styling may be off. The fabric may be faulty. Bought at the end of the season, it may be dated the following year. The particular style may have flooded the market and you'll see yourself coming and going. An unusual button is missing and can't be replaced. The seams may be clipped too close and make alteration a problem. The material may be slightly shaded. The colour may be so odd that you'll have to spend more money on accessories or the dress will be a completely pointless purchase.

A bargain is something I really adore, never tire of wearing; something that makes me feel good, that has given me more than my money's worth in terms of fun and confidence and the pleasure of being dressed.

Can you honestly look into your cupboard without seeing some senseless purchase, clothes you rarely or never wear and only bought because 'they were too good to pass up'? As the Good Book says, 'Let he who is among you without sin cast the first stone!'

When it comes to fashion, I don't believe in compromise. My bargain motto is: 'If it's something you wouldn't buy at the regular price, why buy it now?' I love clothes and when there's something I really want, I believe in getting it exactly as I want to wear it, rather than a reasonable facsimile that's *almost* as good and a bit cheaper. The extra enjoyment is more than worth the extra cost.

Next-best doesn't feel or look right in the end. To get first-best of one item, I would rather live without something else entirely. As in any other situation, compromise leaves nobody really satisfied.

To illustrate my feelings, I'd like to tell you about my two favourite bargains. Both are active in my wardrobe and, if I can help it, will remain on the active list until they fall apart. One is quite expensive, the other quite cheap.

The first is the huge mink gill fur bag my husband bought for me several years ago as a surprise after I had pointedly admired it in a shop window. It cost $200, which is, I agree, a staggering price for a bag. However, I'm about to go into my fifth year with that bag (which breaks down to $40 *per annum*) and I'm still enthusiastic. I love the way it feels. I love the way it looks. I love *it*. I have carried it with tweeds, with early autumn cottons, with a camel's-hair coat. It has literally 'made' countless costumes. As far as I can see, the bag will go on as long as I do, giving me pleasure, playing a decisive role in my wardrobe, making my husband's initial investment a dear one only to me.

The second was something I found myself on a detour through the boys' department of a large store. There, piled on a counter, was an enormous pile of sweaters, navy blue in a very large cable stitch trimmed in white. Imported from Sweden, they were sized for a 14 year-old boy and marked down from $38 to $10. This was a real bargain. The merchandise was perfect and the price was reduced because, understandably, most families do not want to spend so much on a sweater for a rough-and-tumble teenage boy, no matter how beautiful.

This unusual, highly-styled sweater has become an integral part of my year-round wardrobe. I wear it over shorts and slacks in summer, indoors for country week-ends in the winter. It's retained its shape and pattern and, if anything, looks better now than when I got it.

All in all, the best bargain category is accessories. They're safer and fit a more flexible function in the wardrobe. Also worth considering is the fact that classic designs are better than high-style buying. The most rewarding bargain sales are *bona-fide* mark-downs of branded merchandise and perennial styles. Things you might buy at sales include hosiery, gloves, handbags, umbrellas, handkerchiefs, and, sometimes, shoes – if you wear the kind that is being marked down and if they are in timeless lines and in colours that will fill in your shoe wardrobe.

In addition, I'm all for the unexpected, supercilious hat that you can't bear to leave once you've tried it on and around which you can build a wonderful costume. Frivolities come under the heading of things you might have bought at the regular price if you'd seen them but fortunately you didn't until they were reduced.

Here are six questions to ask yourself the next time you go shopping and find a bargain:

1. Is it something I really want?
2. Is it in perfect condition?
3. Is it the right size?
4. Is it still in style?
5. Does it fulfil a wardrobe need?
6. Will it pay its own way as a member of my wardrobe, not just loll as a temporary guest in the back of the cupboard?

Each of your answers will give you a clue as to whether or not the 'bargain' is really a bargain. If it's not something you want, you'll keep making excuses to avoid wearing it – or wear it and wish you hadn't. If it is not in perfect condition, you may have insurmountable problems and waste a lot of time and extra money. Shopworn clothes rarely clean properly. Improper fit means more time and the cost of alterations, which, added up, could have bought you a new dress rather than one that's gone through the mill before you ever wear it.

However much you like it, if it doesn't fit in with your other clothes, do yourself a favour and forget it. The exception, as noted earlier, might be a striking hat around which to assemble a new costume. Can you see yourself wearing it in a particular social or business situation? Style is the most treacherous fashion snare. More often than not, extremes of fashion styling move to the markdown rack at the end of the season faster than traditional classics. Lastly, will it pay its way – or is that wave of emotion gripping you a reluctance to pass up a sensational saving?

Adding up your 'yeses', if you answered 'Yes' to every question then you are a Bargain Shopper First Class, capable of matching wits with provocative signs, seductive marked-down racks, and heady displays of special bargain merchandise. If you had four or five 'Yeses', you can still be trusted to let your good judgment override any sudden whim while you think carefully about the wisdom of such a purchase. Three 'Yeses' marks you a borderline 'bargain buff', which means you make frequent bargain mistakes and have them at home to provoke you.

Less than three 'Yeses' means you should have your cheque-book locked up for a month while you write 500 times, 'I will think before I buy'.

FOURTEEN

Facts and Fancies Plus a Chic Test to Determine your Fashion IQ

I don't think it's too farfetched to predict that someday chic-ology will take its place among the sciences as a key to the emotional well-being of women.

A WOMAN WOULD RATHER BE CALLED 'CHIC' THAN PRETTY.

'Chic' is a word I'm sure Shakespeare would have used – if the word had been part of the English language at the time and if it had been 'chic' to use it. Fundamentally a fashion word today, it expresses more than just clothes or style. It has come to convey a sense of contemporary culture, the ultimate fashion expression for this time and place.

Why this French word has become an American idiom is lost in fashion history. Foreign words are perhaps more exciting than the home-grown product. At a fashion show in Milan I was startled to hear the commentator repeat the word 'zm-m-a-ar-r-t' over and over again in the midst of her rapid-fire Italian commentary. Suddenly I realized that her description of something as 'smart' was the current Italian fashion term for what we in America have borrowed from the French and call 'chic'.

'Chic-ology' is impossible to define. It is the psychology of fashion, meant to be interpreted by each of us in individual terms. I don't think it's too farfetched to predict that someday chic-ology will take its place among the sciences as a key to the emotional well-being of women. The face and form we present to the world are signs of an inner conflict and tranquility. It's not exactly a new idea that looking well makes you feel well. Chic-ology is the means for examining and clarifying your fashion viewpoint.

Perhaps the best way to analyse 'chic' is to say what it is and what it is not. Somewhere in the middle will be the indefinable truth as it applies to you. More than in any other theoretical study, chic-ology must be individually interpreted.

CHIC begins with good taste.
CHIC is organization plus inspiration.
CHIC is a statement of who you are and what you stand for.
CHIC is a picture of you that says more than a thousand words.
CHIC is bearing – the way you walk and move and sit.
CHIC is the image you convey to others.
CHIC is doing something for clothes rather than expecting them to do something for you.
CHIC is appreciation of fabrics, textures, colours.
CHIC is attention to smallest detail.

CHIC is selectivity and the understanding that what may be great for someone else is not necessarily for you.

CHIC is not blind acceptance of fashion fad.

CHIC does not depend on money.

CHIC is classical styling with personal embellishments.

CHIC may be looking different from everyone else or looking the same as everyone else.

CHIC is a personal mood.

CHIC is personal identity, immediately distinguishable.

CHIC is a comprehension of clothes, atmosphere, and surroundings.

CHIC is a custom-made look concocted from the assembly line of fashion.

CHIC is *Instinct* plus *Impulse* plus *Individuality.*

To pursue the subject further, here is a Chic Test based on specific questions of fashion interpretation and viewpoint. Answer *Yes or No* to each and then compare your opinion with the analysis that follows.

1. Do you wear black patent-leather shoes in the winter?

2. For a gala evening, would you wear false eyelashes?

3. With a limited fur budget, would you splurge on a lush fur lining rather than an inexpensive fur coat?

4. To a summer formal would you wear a satin coat over a cotton dress?

5. Do you sometimes build an ensemble around an unusual accessory?

6. Would you wear a tweed dress to a cocktail party?

7. If you had only one piece of real jewellery would you wear it in solitary splendour rather than combine it with imitation?

8. When the new hat styles come out, do you change your hair style to suit them?

9. Would you wear a cocktail-length dress to a formal ball?

10. Would you wear a velvet hat with a summer cotton?

To my way of thinking – and keep in mind that 'chic' is purely personal – the 'chic' answer to all ten questions is *Yes.* And here's why:

1. Black patent shoes are wonderful all year round and add zest to almost any fabric, such as a black-and-brown tweed or a bright red wool for daytime with shiny patent pumps, or embroidered velvet or lavish lace for evening with bare patent sandals.

While patent is traditionally spring footwear, try teaming it with a matching belt with some of your winter costumes. But save patent bags for spring and summer only. For some obscure reason they look out of place in the autumn and winter wardrobe.

2. I adore false eyelashes because they're so frankly fake and can be such fun to flutter on a gay dress-up occasion. While I consider them chic at this writing, I may change my mind about them in six months – or a year or never! However, I do think it's important to consider frivolities as they appear on the fashion scene and wear them appropriately. False eyelashes are gay at an extravagant party. They would be ridiculous in the daytime, casting a grotesque shadow on your face.

3. A fur lining, to me, is more chic than an inexpensive fur coat because you are more aware of the fur enveloping your body; and when you throw back your coat on your chair or drape it around your shoulders, you are silhouetted against a backdrop of luxury.

4. Incongruous combinations add up to chic when the styling is in harmony. I can't think of anything lovelier for a country-club ball than an evening gown of cotton or denim worn with a simple coat of matching or contrasting satin.

5. The chic approach to an ensemble often begins with an accessory such as a fabulous hat or a marvellous bag or a striking piece of jewellery. If you have such an unusual accessory, begin your fashion planning with it rather than tacking it on as an afterthought.

6. Because tweed is essentially a country fabric is no reason to dismiss it from your urban-wardrobe thinking. You can be ultra-chic at a cocktail party in a tweed dress that is styled for the occasion and gaily accessorized. Tweeds can go anywhere combined with fabrics ranging from satin to velvet – as long as the styling is appropriate.

7. I think you add to the importance and splendour of your one solitary jewel by wearing it uncluttered or obscured by lesser

lights. A lone pin on an unadorned bodice expresses such an air of self-assurance!

8. This is the one question where my affirmative answer is theoretical because I haven't changed my hair style in recent years, a circumstance I blame on time. Perhaps before this book is out I shall have restyled my hair because the very fact of its being long and pulled back in a ribbon makes wearing hats very difficult. And I don't think it's possible to be really chic without an active hat wardrobe.

9. Not being Scarlett O'Hara with draperies to whip into ball gowns, you may find yourself in the position of having an invitation to a fancy ball without the time or opportunity to get a ball gown. You can be chic in a cocktail-length dress so long as it is styled in keeping with the formal atmosphere.

10. Velvet with cotton is my favourite combination for midsummer city chic. The simplest town dress becomes an ensemble with the addition of black velvet. Incidentally, for summer evenings, velvet shoes add similar flavour to organza or cotton dance dresses.

❈ ❈ ❈

FIFTEEN

A Glossary and Friendly Guide to Fashion Jargon

'For men, especially, reference to this glossary may make fashion talk more intelligible'

A WORD TO HUSBANDS: *If it's in French, it usually costs more.*

Of course fashion isn't *all* jargon or special names; but like many other fields, it has its own vernacular, some of which has crept into popular usage. Listed here alphabetically are some of the most-used 'fashionese' as found in advertisements and fashion magazines, a fuller knowledge of which will make you a better shopper and enable you to better visualize merchandise shown in print and described in type.

For men, especially, reference to this glossary may make fashion talk more intelligible.

A ACCORDION PLEATS. Knife-narrow, knife-sharp pleats that compress like a closed accordion when off the body.
AERATED YARN. Rayon yarn with a hollow centre that contains inert air which actually makes the fabric breathe.
ALENÇON LACE. Needlepoint lace in a solid pattern set on a net background.
APPLIQUÉ. A pattern of one texture sewed to another, on either contrasting or matching surface, as a matter of pattern interest.
AVONDALE DENIM. Flexible denim fabric that can be styled like silk in styles ranging from active sportswear to glamorous evening gowns.

B BAGUETTE. Rectangular in shape, usually referring to a diamond-cut stone.
BALMACAAN. A loose, flaring overcoat.
BANGLE. A firm, narrow bracelet that slides along the arm.
BARRETTE. A hair clasp.
BENGALINE. A corded fabric with threads of silk crossing ribs of worsted.
BOA. A soft, fluffy neckpiece usually in feathers, fur, or tulle.
BOLERO. A short, loose jacket that stops just above the waist.
BOUCLE. A woven or knitted fabric with a surface that is looped or knotted.
BOUFFANT. Puffed out as if filled with air, such as a fullskirted gown over layers of petticoats.

BOUTIQUE. A shop that specializes in 'items' as opposed to specific merchandise. It's the high-fashion 'drugstore' of the industry.

BRETON. A hat with a rolling brim turned up all round.

BROGUE. Oxford-style walking shoes (not a Celtic accent).

C

CAMISOLE. An undergarment that looks like a dress or an outer garment that looks like an undergarment, it features a neckline cut straight across the chest and slightly above the bustline with straight shoulder straps, usually made of ribbon.

CARTWHEEL. An extra-large hat with an extra-large, even brim.

CELANESE. Maker of synthetic yarns, Acetate, Arnel (ease of care fibre), and Celaperm.

CHANTILLY LACE. Lace design outlined on a delicate net background.

CHAPEAU. Yes, it's a hat!

CHATELAINE. A chain extended across an open jacket or at the waist from which are hung ornamental objects.

CHESTERFIELD. A slim, fly-front coat with a velvet collar.

CHIGNON. A twist of hair worn at the back of the head *or* a cluster of flowers or feathers made to *cover* the twist of hair *or* be worn in place of the twist of hair.

CHINO CLOTH. Cotton-twill dyed in different colours.

CHOKER. A neckpiece, worn high on the throat, that can be made of velvet, jewels, pearls. Can even be a leather dog collar.

CLOCHE. A close-fitting hat that resembles the shape of a bell, which is what *cloche* means in French.

COWL. A monk's hood that is worn draped on the shoulders rather than on the head when applied to women's clothes.

CREPE DE CHINE. A lustrous silk that looks slightly crinkled in texture.

CRINOLINE. A big petticoat, originally made of crinoline fabric, but now synonymous with all stiffened petticoats.

CUBAN HEEL. Medium-height and wide, usually found on a country walking shoe.

CUT VELVET. Velvet with design embossed on its texture.

D

DÉCOLLETAGE. A low-cut neckline.

DÉCOUPAGE. A fabric pattern that has parts of it cut out, such as a sleeve with flower embroidery revealing your arms through the petals.

DIAMANTE. A fabric sparkling with tiny bits of rhinestones.

DIAPHANOUS. Derived from the goddess Diana, this

adjective is used to describe any garment made of filmy, transparent material that floats as it moves.

DICKEY. A detachable shirt front.

DUSTER. A lightweight loose coat, usually unlined.

E ECRU. Light beige or unbleached natural colour.

ÉLAN. A favourite of fashion magazines, it means impetuous and full of spirit.

EMPIRE. Napoleon's Josephine started it in 1804 with its high waistline and short bodice.

ENVELOPE BAG. Small, flat handbag in the elongated, rectangular shape of an envelope.

ETON JACKET. A hip-length, unfitted jacket with a round collar.

F FAGOTTING. Thread, yarn, or ribbon worked into an open seam as a trim.

FAILLE. Slightly glossy silk fabric in a rib weave.

FAWN. A yellowish, dark tan colour.

FICHU. Draped scarf or shawl worn about the shoulders and tied in a knot with the ends hanging loosely down. Or it may be a ruffled collar attached to a blouse or a dress, creating the same effect.

FLOUNCE. A gathered strip of matching or contrasting fabric attached to the bottom of a garment.

FOREST GREEN. Very dark green.

FOULARD. A soft, washable silk with a satiny feel to it. Plain or printed, but usually has tiny figures on a dark or light ground. Sometimes called 'tie silk'. There is a cotton foulard also, but if it is cotton, the label must say so.

FRENCH CUFFS. Double cuffs turned back, having either two or four buttonholes to be fastened together with one link.

FRENCH HEEL. Curved high heel.

FRENCH KID. Very fine quality kid leather.

FRENCH SEAM. Narrow seam stitched first on right then on wrong side, concealing rough edges.

FROCK. Fancy name for 'dress'.

FUCHSIA. Purplish-red.

FULLY-FASHIONED. Adjective describing a garment such as stockings or a sweater that is knitted flat and shaped by dropping of stitches.

G GAMIN. Descriptive of a small, vivacious woman with a mischievous twinkle and clothes designed expressly to convey this feeling.

GANT. French for glove.

GEORGETTE CREPE. Sheer crepe.

GLEN PLAID. Abbreviation for Glenurquhart, a Scottish clan plaid. It is always in muted colours.

GOSSAMER. Sheer; very thin.

H

HAUTE COUTURE. Actually means high fashion and refers to the leading dressmakers of Paris and to extreme and expensive styles.

HELIOTROPE. Purple-blue colour.

HUNTER'S GREEN. Slightly yellowish dark green.

HYACINTH. Lavender-blue colour.

I

INVERTED PLEAT. A box pleat reversed.

IRIDESCENT. Descriptive of fabric made of contrasting colour fillings which give off a changing-colour effect when the fabric moves.

IRISH LACE. Usually a shamrock or rose design surrounded by mesh.

IRISH LINEN. A fine, lightweight linen.

J

JABOT. A frill or ruffle, lace or lace-trimmed, which cascades down the front of the bodice and fastens at the neckline.

JACQUARD. A fabric with an intricate figured weave.

JAPANESE EMBROIDERY. Elaborate silk embroidery in satin-stitch.

JAUNE. French word meaning 'yellow'.

JEUNE FILLE. Actually means 'young girl', but applies to styles that are youthful.

K

KASHA. Soft silky wool mixed with goat hair on a twill weave.

KHAKI. Olive drab.

KID. Tanned goat leather.

KIDSKIN. Baby goatskin.

KIMONO SLEEVES. Sleeve cut in one piece with the body of the garment.

KOLINSKY. Asiatic mink.

L

LAMÉ. Delicate fabric woven of gold or silver threads mixed with silk or other fibres.

LARKSPUR. A light blue colour with a slightly greenish tinge.

LASTEX. Trade name of an elastic yarn that is good for knitting and weaving.

LATEX. A milky plant substance from which wearable rubber is made.

LAVABLE. Usually found inside French gloves, it means 'washable'.

LAWN. Fine, soft, sheer cotton.

LEATHERETTE. A paper or cloth imitation of leather grain.

LEGHORN. Finely plaited straw.

LINDE. Remarkable synthetic star sapphires and star rubies.

LISLE. Hard-twisted cotton thread.

LODEN. Coarse woollen waterproof cloth of Tyrolean design; also used generically as a colour of green: 'loden green'.

LUREX. Synthetic metallic yarn, used very much like lamé thread.

M MACKINAW. A short bulky coat with a plaid lining inspired by lumberjacks.

MACKINTOSH. A waterproofed coat.

MAGENTA. Purplish-red colour.

MAILLOT. A tight one-piece bathing suit, usually knitted.

MAQUILLAGE. French for 'make-up', the term is used by some American cosmetics and can be seen on imported cosmetics.

MARABOU. Soft tail- and wing feathers of the African stork.

MAROON. A dull red colour, the result of black mixed with red.

MARQUISE. A pointed oval-shaped gem, usually diamond or rhinestone.

MARQUISETTE. An open-faced fabric of silk or cotton, sometimes both combined.

MATARA. Dark brown sealskin.

MATT FINISH. Dull, unglazed surface.

MERINO. Fine wool from Merino sheep.

MIDNIGHT BLUE. The darkest possible blue.

MIDRIFF. Physically it's the part of your body between the chest and abdomen. Fashion-wise, it may mean a style that emphasizes the midriff by a band or treatment that encircles the waist.

MOIRÉ. A watered or clouded effect on a soft fabric.

MOLESKIN. Soft, iridescent fur that takes well to colour.

MONK'S CLOTH. A heavy, crude fabric with a basket weave.

MOUSSELINE DE SOIE. A transparent gauzelike silk fabric in an even weave with a firm finish.

MULE. A backless bedroom slipper.

N NINON. A stout French chiffon, stiffer than regular chiffon, with a clear, transparent surface.

NORFOLK JACKET. A belted, single-breasted jacket.

OBI. A broad Japanese cummerbund.

OPERA PUMP. Plain, untrimmed classic pump.

PAGODA SLEEVES. Those which are fitted at the armhole and grow progressively wider to the opening.

PASSEMENTERIE. Heavy braid embroideries and edgings.

PEAU DE SOIE. A firm, soft, durable silk in a twill weave which has a dull satin-like finish.

PEIGNOIR. In France it's a terry-cloth robe used instead of a towel after a bath. In the United States it's a negligee.

PIN TUCK. The narrowest possible tuck.

PINWALE. Very narrow-rib corduroy.

PLATINA. Very light beige fur, the name coming from platinum.

PLISSÉ. French for 'gathers', 'pleats', or 'folds'.

PLISSÉ CREPE. Crepe fabric with a puckered, seersucker finish.

PRIMROSE. Greenish-yellow or reddish-yellow colour.

RAGLAN. Loose overcoat with armhole seams extending from the neck.

REDINGOTE. A three-quarter or full-length dress or coat worn open over a dress or matching slip.

REMNANT. More than a half-yard of left-over fabric. Less than a half-yard is classified as 'scraps'.

ROMAN STRIPES. Usually bold stripes in a series of several contrasting colours.

RUBBERIZED. Coated or covered with rubber.

RUBBER-PROOFED. Combined with rubber in the making of the fabric.

SAILCLOTH. The heavy quality is used for sails, tents, and home furnishing, the lightweight is used for sportswear.

SATEEN. Cotton fabric with a satin finish.

SCHIFFLI. A machine-made embroidery that looks like hand embroidery and has made elaborate embroidery possible in moderate-priced fashions. Prohibitive if done by hand, lavish Schiffli embroidery can cover the fabric or add decorative touches.

SHADOW LACE. Indistinct lace designs, machine- or handmade.

SHIRRING. Three or more rows of gathers.

SHOT SILK. Fabric woven with different-colour warp and weft, causing the tint to vary as the fabric moves.

SKIMMER. A sailor hat, usually straw, with a wide brim and flat crown.

SLIPOVER. Sweater or other garment with no side or back opening.

SLIPPER SATIN. A very strong, durable, closely woven satin.

SPANISH LACE. Made in Spain in a flat, floral pattern.

SPENCER. A short jacket, often fur-trimmed.

SUMMER ERMINE. Either white ermine dyed beige or brown weasel fur.

SUNBURST PLEATS. Accordion pleats in a flared effect.

SUPIMA. Luxury cotton fabric that is durable, lustrous, and washes beautifully.

SURAH. Soft lightweight twill fabric of silk or wool.

T TAUPE. Dark grey colour with brown tones.

TERRA-COTTA. Reddish-orange colour.

TON. French for describing the prevailing high fashion, often used in fashion magazines as a descriptive word.

TOQUE. A small, close-fitting brimless hat.

TREWS. Tartan trousers.

TRICOT. Fabric that is knitted or woven to look knitted.

TWILL. Fabric woven so as to produce ribs or diagonal lines.

U ULSTER. A long, loose, heavy coat.

UNCUT VELVET. Velvet fabric with the woven loops intact, which makes a plushier surface.

UNDRESSED KID. Kid leather finished on the flesh side by a suede process.

UNPRESSED PLEATS. Folds that form pleats but are not stitched or pressed flat.

V VAT-DYED. Colour-processing that makes the fabric fast to sun and water.

VENT. A slash in the fabric of a garment partway up a seam.

VICUÑA. Very expensive fabric made from the wool of the Llama-like vicuña which grazes in the Andes.

In addition, here are two of my favourite Seventh Avenue expressions which you may never see or hear – unless you visit the New York Garment Centre:

GREEN ROOM. A payday expression meaning 'the bank'.
SIGNER OF THE SMALL PAY CHEQUES. *The boss!*